Anatomy of a Conversion

The Message and Mission of John & Charles Wesley

Anatomy of a Conversion

Philip S. Watson

Foreword by Robert G. Tuttle, Jr.

Anatomy of a Conversion

Francis Asbury Press is an imprint of Zondervan Publishing House,
1415 Lake Drive, S.E., Grand Rapids, Michigan 49506

Library of Congress Cataloging in Publication Data

Watson, Philip S. (Philip Saville)
Anatomy of a conversion : the message and mission of John and Charles Wesley / Philip S. Watson.
p. cm.
Previously presented as the introduction to the Message of the Wesleys by the author.
Includes bibliographical references.
ISBN 0-310-74991-3
1. Wesley, John, 1703-1791. 2. Wesley, Charles, 1707-1788. 3. Methodist Church–England–Clergy–Biography. 4. Methodist Church–Doctrines. I. Title.
BX8495.W5W28 1990
287'.092'2–dc20
[B] 89-38796
CIP

Printed in the United States of America

90 91 92 93 94 95 / CH / 10 9 8 7 6 5 4 3 2 1

Contents

Philip S. Watson (1909–1983)

Philip S. Watson was one of the world's major Wesley scholars. Ordained by the Methodist Church in Britain in 1934, he joined the faculty of Garrett Theological Seminary (now Garrett-Evangelical Theological Seminary) in Evanston, Illinois, in 1960. A year later he was elected the first Harris Franklin Rall Professor of Systematic Theology. In 1973 Dr. Watson retired and returned to England.

Professor Watson distinguished himself as scholar and teacher. His intensive research into the writings of both Martin Luther and John Wesley resulted in his wide reputation as lecturer and authority on the two men and their movements.

Dr. Watson was born in Bradford, Yorkshire. He received the B. A. degree (First Class Honors in classics) from St. John's College, University of Durham, in 1931 and an M. A. degree from Durham in 1934. Wesley House, Cambridge, granted him another B. A. degree (again with First Class Honors) in 1934 and an M. A. degree in 1939. He did further study in patristics and the Reformation at Tübingen and Lund. Wesley House, the University of Glasgow, and Ohio Wesleyan University each honored him with a Doctor of Divinity degree.

Before accepting the post at Garrett Theological Seminary, he served two pastoral appointments in Britain and was Professor of Systematic Theology and Philosophy of Religion at Handsworth College, Birmingham; and Professor of Systematic and Pastoral Theology at Wesley House, Cambridge.

Dr. Watson died in England on June 8, 1983.

Foreword

This small book is Philip Watson's introduction to his own valuable *The Message of the Wesleys*. Here he writes that "the most important thing about the Wesleys is that they were men of God, men who knew God and knew how to lead others to the knowledge of God. . . ."[1] Philip Watson himself was such a man. A colleague and I recently sat reminiscing about our old mentor and friend. We remembered his availability. Professor Watson, even in the midst of deadline and crisis had a calm centeredness about him that revealed a quiet ministry (an "evangelism") in personhood. The Wesleys would be proud to have his name in association with their own.

A brilliant man (with two earned degrees from Cambridge), Professor Watson was equally at home with the Reformation, be it English (via Ridley and Latimer) or Continental (his book on Martin Luther, *Let God Stand,* is a classic). As a student, I probably worked harder in his courses than in any other (although for many of us simply pleasing him was more important than the grade). He was tough but he was fair. His book *The Message of the Wesleys* is also tough and fair. It is tough in that he allows the Wesleys to surface as men, bold and vulnerable. It is fair in that he prevents the reader from interpreting the Wesleys purely in light of one's own passion alone. A balanced approach gives significant exposure to both the Wesleys as preachers/evangelists, theologians, organizers, hymn writers, social reformers, and men of spiritual integrity deeply committed to "spreading Scriptural holiness throughout the land." Professor Watson's Introduction to this extremely helpful anthology could outlive him (he died in 1983) a hundred years.

The Introduction itself, entitled "Anatomy of a Conversion," is written in two parts: "Discovery of a Message" and "Fulfilment of a Mission." "Discovery of a Message" describes the evangelical conversions of both the Wesleys (using for the most part primary sources) in a way that is honest and sympathetic. For example, Professor Watson avoids the trap of placing too much emphasis upon the well-worn phrase "heart strangely warmed" when writing of John Wesley's conversion. He does this by allowing John to speak for himself without any undue attempt to "clean up" after someone else's religious experience. After commenting that "[John] Wesley's Methodist descendants, all too often talk about Wesley's warmed heart without any reference to the fire that warmed it," he highlights the major issues at stake but then includes nearly a full page of Wesley's own Journal so that readers can judge for themselves.[2]

In the section, "Fulfilment of a Mission," Professor Watson's true genius becomes most apparent. This is as good an introduction to the Wesley's practice, teaching, and method of revival as can be found anywhere. It is clear and concise, at once challenging and inspirational. For example, the commentary on John Wesley's simple "fourfold formula" for teaching (all need to be saved, can be saved, can know that they are saved, and can be saved to the uttermost) can give the reader a valuable insight into how *both* the Wesleys went about doing theology in the midst of their ongoing ministry (selections from Charles' hymns punctuate all of this as well).

One of the principal aims of Professor Watson's Introduction is to move readers into primary sources so that they can discover for themselves the wealth of material so incredibly relevant for the church today. In light of the new Bicentennial Edition of *The Works of John Wesley* now being published, this Introduction can be used as a timely catalyst for plumbing the depths of untold treasures.

Professor Watson states in his Introduction, "There is not much that is new—fundamentally new—under the sun."[3] The longer I live the more sense that statement makes to me. Today people still need to be saved; the Wesleys speak to that. Today people still need to fear sin as much as death or hell; the Wesleys speak to that. Today people still oppress each other; the Wesleys speak to that. Today the church still needs fellowship and accountability; the Wesleys speak to that. Today love is still the beginning and end of the Christian faith; the Wesleys speak to that—and to much, much more!

Whether in church school or seminary classroom, this reprint of a classic introduction to the message of the Wesleys should find wide distribution as, one hopes, it helps to launch a whole new generation of Wesley enthusiasts who will continue to pray along with the rest of us: "God, do it again!"

Robert G. Tuttle, Jr., Ph.D.
E. Stanley Jones Professor of Evangelism
Garrett-Evangelical Theological Seminary
Evanston, Illinois

Notes

[1] Philip S. Watson, *The Message of the Wesleys: A Reader of Instruction and Devotion* (Grand Rapids, Zondervan/Francis Asbury Press, 1984), xvi.
[2] Ibid., 6.
[3] Ibid., xvi.

List of Works Cited

Hildebrandt, F., ed. *The Wesley Hymn Book*, London, 1960; Kansas City, Mo., 1963.

The Methodist Hymnal. Official Hymnal of the Methodist Church. Nashville, 1932.

The Methodist Hymn Book. London, 1933.

Wesley, Charles. *The Journal of the Rev. Charles Wesley, M.A.*, ed. Thomas Jackson. London, 1849. 2 vols.

———. *The Journal of the Rev. Charles Wesley, M.A.*, 1736-39, ed. John Telford. London, 1909.

Wesley, John. *The Journal of the Rev. John Wesley, A.M.*, Std. edn., ed. Nehemiah Curnock. London, 1938. 8 vols.

———. *The Letters of the Rev. John Wesley, A.M.*, Std. edn., ed. John Telford. London, 1931. 8 vols.

———. *Wesley's Standard Sermons,* ed. and annot. Edward H. Sugden. London, 1921-56. 2 vols.

———. *The Works of the Rev. John Wesley, A.M.,* with the Last Corrections of the Author, ed. Thomas Jackson. London, 1829-31. 14 vols.

———. *A Collection of Hymns for the Use of the People Called Methodists.* London, 1780. Revised with a new suppl., London, Wesleyan Conference Office, 1876.

——— and Charles Wesley. *Hymns on the Lord's Supper.* Bristol, 1745. Reprinted in *The Eucharistic Hymns of John and Charles Wesley* by J. E. Rattenbury, London, 1948.

Abbreviations

AMH	*The* (American) *Methodist Hymnal*
CW	Charles Wesley
CWJ(J)	*The Journal of the Rev. Charles Wesley, M.A.* (Jackson ed.)
CWJ(T)	*The Journal of the Rev. Charles Wesley, M.A.* (Telford ed.)
HLS	*Hymns on the Lord's Supper*
HPCM	*A Collection of Hymns for the Use of the People Called Methodists*
HPCM(S)	Supplement to *HPCM*
JW	John Wesley
JWJ	*The Journal of the Rev. John Wesley, A.M.*
L	*The Letters of the Rev. John Wesley, A.M.*
Large Minutes	"Minutes of Several Conversations between the Rev. Mr. Wesley and Others"
MHB	*The* (British) *Methodist Hymn Book*
Minutes	"Minutes of Some Late Conversations between the Rev. Mr. Wesley and Others"
S	Sermon
SS	*Wesley's Standard Sermons*
W	*The Works of the Rev. John Wesley, A.M.*
WHB	*The Wesley Hymn Book*

INTRODUCTION

Anatomy of a Conversion

* * *

I

Discovery of a Message

PENTECOST AT ALDERSGATE

On a day late in February, 1738, in a lodging in Oxford, two young men were engaged in serious conversation. One of them, an Anglican clergyman, lay in bed suffering from a severe attack of pleurisy. His name was Charles Wesley. The other, who had come to visit his sick friend, was a minister of the Moravian Church, who was intending to go shortly as a missionary to America. His name was Peter Böhler.

The conversation turned very soon to the deep things of the Christian faith and life, and Peter Böhler led it to the point where he asked Charles Wesley what reason he had for hoping to be saved. The answer Charles gave was simple and direct. He said: "Because I have used my best endeavours to serve God." At this Peter Böhler shook his head, and although he made no spoken comment, his silence was more eloquent than words. After he had gone, Charles Wesley wrote in his *Journal:* "I thought him very uncharitable, saying in my heart, 'What, are not my endeavours a sufficient ground of hope? Would he rob me of my endeavours? I have nothing else to trust to.'"[1]

Charles Wesley's attitude was very human—all too human. "I've done my best," people say, "I've done my best, and what more can God require of me?" Yet few people have such a best, such endeavours to rely on, as Charles Wesley had.

Ten years or so earlier, he had resolved to devote all his time and talents to the service of God. He had gathered around him a few like-minded friends, including his own brother, John, and together they had formed a little religious society, which soon became mockingly known as the Holy Club. They had pledged themselves to daily Bible-study and prayer and to weekly attendance at Holy Communion. They had given themselves unsparingly to works of charity—visiting the sick and those in prison, feeding the hungry, clothing the naked, and teaching the children of the poor. They had also earned themselves a certain amount of unpopularity by their devotion to such a rigorous role of life and had been called by a variety of derisive names, such as Bible-moths, Sacramentarians, and *Methodists.*[2] And in all this Charles Wesley had played his part; indeed he had done more. Of his own free will he had refused an offer of flourishing estates in Ireland, owned by a childless cousin who wished to make him his heir. Instead he had gone, with his brother and two other friends from the Holy Club, to Georgia in order to serve God under the rude and rigorous conditions of the newly opened British colony there. They went, as John explains, "not to avoid want, God having given us plenty of temporal blessings, nor to gain riches or honour, which we trust he will ever enable us to look on as no other than dung and dross; but singly this—to save our souls, to live wholly to the glory of God."[3]

Surely, then, Charles Wesley had reason to say that he had "used his best endeavours to serve God"; and what endeavours they were! So was not Peter Böhler "very uncharitable" to suggest, even by silence, that he had no ground of hope for salvation in them? What had Peter in mind?

If he had spoken, his argument might have run something like this: "Charles, that is sheer pride. Indeed, it's worse, it's unbelief; for it's entirely contrary to the gospel. You know what St. Paul says: 'By grace you have been saved through faith; and this is not your own doing, it is the gift of God—not because of works, lest any man should boast. For we are his workmanship, created in Christ Jesus for good works'—*for* them, Charles, not *by* them!—'which God prepared beforehand that we should walk in them.' Do you really think that man can purchase his salvation by his good works and endeavours? Is God's kingdom put up for sale, like wares on a market-stall? If it were, do you really think you would have enough to be able to pay for it?" (Charles Wesley did not think so, of course; he only hoped, and rather uncertainly at that. He was far from sure, as many people are today.)

However, Peter Böhler's argument would go on: "If you have used your time and talents in the service of God, does this deserve praise or reward from him? Doesn't our Lord tell us something about this?

'When you have done all that is commanded you, say, "We are unworthy servants; we have only done our duty.'" After all, who gave you your time and talents? To whom do you owe them? Don't you owe your very existence, your life, with all your powers of body and soul, everything you have and are—don't you owe it to God alone, who created you? 'It is he that hath made us, and not we ourselves.' Shall *we,* then, who did not and could not give ourselves even our earthly, temporal life, imagine that we can rely on ourselves for eternal life and blessedness? How can we, especially when we remember how imperfect our service of God has been? How much we have left undone that we ought to have done! How often we have done what we ought not to have done! No, Charles, there is no health in us that we should look to ourselves for salvation. We must look to Christ, and to God in Christ, to his mercy, his forgiving and renewing grace, and to that alone."

Not until the beginning of May did Peter Böhler convince Charles Wesley of all this—though some weeks earlier he had persuaded John, with whom he had also been in touch since February. By this time Charles was lodging in London. He had still not fully recovered from his illness, and although he was at last persuaded of the truth of Peter Böhler's teaching, he had still not made it truly his own. He was "convinced of unbelief." For it is possible to believe, even fervently, in the doctrine of salvation by faith without having that faith in Christ of which the doctrine speaks, the faith that saves. This was John Wesley's situation, too, for he also was convinced that the doctrine was true and was preaching it regularly at the time, while knowing that he himself was without saving faith. Like Charles, he was convinced of unbelief.

John appears to have been more prepared than his brother for Peter Böhler's message as a result in particular of experiences he had had with other Moravians both on shipboard and in Georgia. During a violent storm at sea, for example, he observed that a group of Moravian emigrants alone among both passengers and crew seemed unafraid; and he tells us: "I asked one of them afterwards, 'Were you not afraid?' He answered, 'I thank God, no.' I asked, 'But were not your women and children afraid?' He replied mildly, 'No; our women and children are not afraid to die.'"[4]

This reply shook John Wesley even more than the storm had done. Then, a few days after his landing in Georgia, some searching questions were put to him during a conversation he had with another Moravian, August Gottlieb Spangenberg, that still further disturbed him. "[He asked me]! 'Does the Spirit of God bear witness with your spirit that you are a child of God?' I was surprised, and knew not what to answer. He observed it and asked, 'Do you know Jesus Christ?' I paused, and said, 'I know he is the Saviour of the world.' 'True,' replied he, 'but do you know he has saved you?' I answered, 'I hope he has died to save me.' He only added, 'Do you know yourself?' I said, 'I do.' But I fear they were vain words."[5]

John Wesley had thus long been questioning his own spiritual state before he met Peter Böhler, and yet he was far from easily persuaded by Peter, as his *Journal* shows. He says:

In my return to England, January 1738, being in imminent danger of death, and very uneasy on that account, I was strongly convinced that the cause of that uneasiness was unbelief; and that the gaining a true, living faith was the "one thing needful" for me. But still I fixed not this faith on its right object. I meant only faith in God, not faith in or through Christ. Again, I knew not that I was wholly void of this faith; but only thought I had not enough of it. So that when Peter Böhler, whom God prepared for me as soon as I came to London, affirmed of true faith in Christ (which is but one) that it had those two fruits inseparably attending it, "dominion over sin and constant peace from a sense of forgiveness," I was quite amazed, and looked upon it as a new gospel. If this was so, it was clear I had not faith. But I was not willing to be convinced of this. Therefore I disputed with all my might, and laboured to prove that faith might be where these were not; for all the scriptures relating to this I had been long since taught to construe away. Besides, I well saw no one could, in the nature of things, have such a sense of forgiveness and not *feel* it. But I felt it not. If, then, there was no faith without this, all my pretensions to faith dropped at once.[6]

It was, he tells us, on March 5 that he was first "clearly convinced of unbelief, of the want of that faith whereby we are saved";[7] and yet he was still slow to accept what Peter Böhler maintained concerning faith as a gift and work of God. In particular, he "could not understand how this faith should be given in a moment; how a man could *at once* be thus turned from darkness to light, from sin and misery to righteousness and joy in the Holy Ghost."[8] He seems not to have been fully convinced of this until near the end of April, when (in company with Charles) he met Peter Böhler once more.

When I met Peter Böhler again [he writes], he consented to put the dispute upon the issue which I desired, namely, Scripture and experience. I first consulted the Scripture. But when I set aside the glosses of men and simply considered the words of God, comparing them together, endeavouring to illustrate the obscure by the plainer passages, I found they all made against me, and was forced to retreat to my last hold, "that experience would never agree with the *literal interpretation* of those scriptures. Nor could I therefore allow it to be true, till I found some living witnesses of it." He replied, he could show me such at any time; if I desired it, the next day. And accordingly the next day he came again with three others, all of whom testified, of their own personal experience, that a true, living faith in Christ is inseparable from a sense of pardon for all past and freedom from all present sins. They added with one mouth that this faith was the gift, the free gift of God; and that he would surely bestow it upon every soul who earnestly and perseveringly sought it. I was now thoroughly convinced; and, by the grace of God, I resolved to seek it unto the end, (1) by absolutely renouncing all dependence, in whole or in part, upon *my own* works or righteousness; on which I had really grounded my hope of salvation, though I knew it not, from my youth up; (2) by adding to the constant use of all the other means of grace continual prayer for this very thing, justifying, saving faith, a full reliance on the blood of Christ shed for *me;* a trust in him as *my* Christ, as *my* sole justification, sanctification and redemption.[9]

Let us, however, now return to Charles Wesley, still a sick man in his lodging in London. On May 17, he received a visit from a new Moravian friend, William Holland, who brought with him a copy of Martin Luther's *Commentary on St. Paul's Epistle to the Galatians.* They read it together, then afterwards Charles read it alone. He found it, he says, "nobly full of faith,"[10] and he read it eagerly, himself longing and labouring to believe. He recognised in Luther's teaching a doctrine identical with that of the Articles and Homilies of his own Church and was astonished that he should ever have thought this a new doctrine.[11] Then at length he came to Luther's exposition of Galatians 2:20, where St. Paul speaks of "the Son of God who loved me, and gave himself for me." Here is part of what he read:

Who is this "me"? Even I, wretched and damnable sinner, so dearly beloved of the Son of God that he gave himself for me. If I, then, through works or merits could have loved the Son of God, and so come unto him, what needed he to deliver himself for me?... If I, being a wretch and a damned sinner, could be redeemed by any other price, what needed the Son of God to be given for me? But because there was no other price, either in heaven or in earth, but Christ the Son of God, therefore it was most necessary that he should be delivered for me. Moreover, this he did of inestimable love; for Paul says, "who loved me." For he delivered neither sheep, ox, gold, nor silver, but even God himself entirely and wholly, "for me," even for "me," I say, a miserable and wretched sinner.

Read therefore with great vehemency these words, "ME" and "FOR ME," and so inwardly practise with thyself, that thou with a sure faith mayest conceive and print this "ME" in thy heart, and apply it unto thyself, not doubting but that thou art of the number of those to whom this "ME" belongeth; also that Christ hath not only loved Peter and Paul, and given himself for them, but that the same grace also which is comprehended in this "ME" as well pertaineth and cometh unto us as unto them. For as we cannot deny but that we are all sinners, and are constrained to say that through the sin of Adam we are all lost [and] subject to the wrath and judgment of God, so can we not deny but that Christ died for our sins, that he might make us righteous. For he died, not to justify the righteous, but the unrighteous, and to make them the friends and children of God, and inheritors of all heavenly gifts. Therefore, when I feel and confess myself to be a sinner through Adam's transgression, why should I not say that I am made righteous through the righteousness of Christ, especially when I hear that he loved me and gave himself for me?[12]

That was what Charles read, and the message of it struck home. By prayer and meditation and by conversing with Christian friends, he sought to follow Luther's counsel and apply St. Paul's word to himself. Three days later he was enabled to do so, and on Sunday, May 21, the day of Pentecost, he rose from his convalescent couch, freed from the pain and weakness of his pleurisy and thoroughly happy in God. That, however, was not the end of the story but only a new beginning, as we shall see.

Late the following Wednesday evening, an excited little group of people made their way to Charles's lodging. John was at their head, and he burst in on his surprised and overjoyed brother, exclaiming: "I believe!"[13]—as if he said, "I too believe, Charles; I now believe as you do"—for he had heard, two days before, what he calls "the surprising news that my brother had found rest to his soul."[14]

John had come from the meeting of that religious society in Aldersgate Street, to which, as he tells us, he had gone "very unwillingly." He had been in the same distress of soul as Charles. He was convinced of the truth of the doctrine of salvation by faith and, at the same time, of his own lack of faith—"convinced of unbelief." He was preaching faith to others but not possessing it himself. In Aldersgate Street, however, he heard someone read Luther's *Preface to the Epistle to the Romans,* and Luther clinched matters for him as he had already done for Charles. "About a quarter before nine, while he was describing the change which God works in the heart through faith in Christ, I felt my heart strangely warmed. I felt I did trust in Christ, Christ alone for salvation; and an assurance was given me that he had taken away *my* sins, even *mine,* and saved *me* from the law of sin and death."[15]

Wesley's Methodist descendants, I fear, all too often talk about Wesley's warmed heart without any reference to the fire that warmed it. They even exhort People to warmth, as if a man could generate his own heat, instead of speaking words aflame with the love of God in Christ, which might kindle an answering fire. Let us then listen to some of the words that John Wesley heard that night:

Doing the works of the law [Luther says] and fulfilling the law are two very different things. The work of the law is everything that one does or can do, towards keeping the law of his own free will or by his own powers. But since under all these works and along with them there remains in the heart dislike for the law, and the compulsion to keep it, these works are all wasted and of no value. That is what St. Paul means when he says: "By the works of the law no man becomes righteous before God." To fulfil the law, however, is to do its works with pleasure and love, and to live a godly and good life of one's own accord, without the compulsion of the law. This pleasure and love for the law is put into the heart by the Holy Ghost. But the Holy Ghost is not given except in, with and by faith in Jesus Christ. And faith does not come save only through God's word or gospel, which preaches Christ, that he is God's Son and a man, and has died and risen again for our sakes.

Hence it comes that faith alone makes righteous and fulfils the law; for out of Christ's merit it brings the Spirit, and the Spirit makes the heart glad and free as the law requires that it shall be. Faith, however, is a divine work in us. It changes us and makes us to be born anew of God (John 1.); it kills the old Adam and makes altogether new and different men, in heart and spirit and mind and powers, and it brings with it the Holy Ghost. O, it is a living, busy, active, mighty thing, this faith, and so it is impossible for it not to do good works incessantly. It does not ask whether there are good works to do, but before the question rises it has already done them, and is always at the doing of them.

Faith is a living, daring confidence in God's grace, so sure and certain that a man would stake his life on it a thousand times. This confidence in God's grace and knowledge of it, makes a man glad and bold and happy in dealing with God and with all his creatures; and this is the work of the Holy Ghost in faith. Hence a man is ready and glad, without compulsion, to do good to everyone, to serve everyone, to suffer everything, in love and praise of God, who has shown him this grace; and thus it is impossible to separate works from faith, as impossible as to separate heat and light from fire.[16]

"As impossible as to separate heat and light from fire."That is why the Wesleys' evangelical conversion, or pentecostal experience, or call it what you will, was not the end but only a new beginning. "I began," writes John in his *Journal,* "to pray with all my might for those who had in a more especial manner despitefully used me and persecuted me. I then testified openly to all there what I now first felt in my heart."[17] That was the immediate and spontaneous fruit of the warning of his heart.

John and Charles Wesley now no longer merely hoped for salvation; they had received it and were sure of it. And they were sure, not on the basis of their own good works and "best endeavours," not on the basis of their own righteousness, but on the basis of God's righteousness, God's work through Christ for them and in them. Not that their assurance always remained equally clear and strong, and they sometimes held the gift of God with weak and trembling hands, as we shall see; but they never afterwards let it go. Nor did they cease from their good works and their devoted service of God and man. On the contrary, they only now truly began. They began their lifelong, tireless pursuit of those "good works which God had prepared beforehand" for them to walk in.

Not for a moment did they leave off any of the tasks they had assumed before—their Bible-study and constant prayer and frequent attendance at Holy Communion, their visiting of the sick and those in prison, feeding the hungry, clothing the naked, teaching, preaching, exhorting, rebuking, comforting. But all was now done with a new heart and mind. They were not now seeking anxiously to save their own souls but rather yielding themselves in grateful obedience to God, to be instruments in his hand for the salvation of others; and this, not by their own "best endeavours," but by the limitless resources and mighty power of the Holy Ghost given unto them. It was no longer their own work, but God's work in and through them.

Sometimes modern Christians look back wistfully to the days of the Wesleys and the Evangelical Revival and lament that "times have changed" and "things don't happen now as they did then." That is just what John Wesley said when Peter Böhler was trying to convince him of the reality of salvation by faith. Even when he was persuaded that this was the teaching of the New Testament and the experience of the first Christians, he argued: "Thus, I grant, God wrought in the first ages of Christianity; but times are changed. What reason have I to believe he works in the same manner now?" But he was "beat out of this retreat," he says, "by the concurring evidence of several living witnesses, who testified God had thus wrought in themselves."[18] Then, on May 24, he found confirmation in his own experience of what the New Testament and the "living witnesses" had taught him. He found that although the times might have changed, God had not nor had God's plan of salvation, and the same resources that were available to the first Christians were available also to him. And the same resources are available still today for us, by the same grace of God and the same "living, busy, active, mighty faith," the all-victorious faith of Paul, of Luther, of Peter Böhler and the Wesleys.

This faith, of which the seeds were first planted by our Lord in the days of his flesh, came to full flower first at Pentecost, when the Holy Spirit was poured out on the Apostles. It has withered and revived countless times since then, and it blossomed again at Whitsuntide, the anniversary of Pentecost, in May, 1738, in the experience of John and Charles Wesley. To celebrate it, Charles wrote a hymn, which the two brothers sang together after John's confession of faith on the evening of May 24. In these verses they expressed both their gratitude to God and their dedication to the mission that was to occupy them for the rest of their lives.

Where shall my wondering soul begin?
  How shall I all to heaven aspire?
A slave redeemed from death and sin,
  A brand plucked from eternal fire,
How shall I equal triumphs raise,
  Or sing my great Deliverer's praise?

O how shall I the goodness tell,
  Father, which thou to me hast showed?
That I, a child of wrath and hell,
  I should be called a child of God,
Should know, should feel, my sins forgiven,
  Blest with this antepast of heaven!

And shall I slight my Father's love?
  Or basely fear his gifts to own?
Unmindful of his favours prove?
  Shall I, the hallowed cross to shun,
Refuse his righteousness to impart,
  By hiding it within my heart?

Outcasts of men, to you I call,
  Harlots and publicans and thieves!
He spreads his arms to embrace you all;
  Sinners alone his grace receives;
No need of him the righteous have;
  He came the lost to seek and save.

Come, O my guilty brethren, come,
  Groaning beneath your load of sin!
His bleeding heart shall make you room,
  His open side shall take you in;
He calls you now, invites you home;
  Come, O my guilty brethren, come![19]

PILGRIMS' PROGRESS

That the experience of John and Charles Wesley in May, 1738, was a decisive turning-point in their lives is indisputable. The traditional understanding of it as the authentic starting-point of the Methodist Revival is also entirely proper. Yet its essential significance has often been obscured, especially when undue attention has been paid to the temperature of John Wesley's "strangely warmed" heart. Methodists have in consequence often been accused (and not always unjustly) of teaching "salvation by feeling." They have even at times appeared to substitute a rather vague, general notion of "religious experience" for faith in Jesus Christ. But such charges cannot lie against the Wesleys.

In a letter written in 1771, John says: "Many years since, I saw that 'without holiness no man shall see the Lord.' I began following after it, and inciting all with whom I had any intercourse to do the same. Ten years after, God gave me a clearer view than I had before of the way how to attain this—namely, by faith in the Son of God. And immediately I declared to all, 'We are saved from sin, we are made holy, by faith.'"[20] The same point is made elsewhere, thus:

> *Q. What was the rise of Methodism, so called?*
>
> *A. In 1729, two young men, reading the Bible, saw they could not be saved without holiness, followed after it, and incited others to do so. In 1737, they saw holiness comes by faith. They saw likewise that men are justified before they are sanctified; but still holiness was their point. God then thrust them out, utterly against their will, to raise a holy people.*[21]

What this means can be expressed as follows: (1) From the inception of the Holy Club (and in John's case even earlier[22]) both the Wesleys were engaged in the pursuit of holiness. By holiness they meant nothing else but the love of God and man, or "the mind that was in Christ." They were seeking to fulfil the great twofold commandment: "Thou shalt love the Lord thy God with all thy heart and mind and soul and strength; and thou shalt love thy neighbour as thyself." (2) But they were seeking to cultivate this love in themselves by their own devotion and "best endeavours." Just as Luther had sought to fulfil the commandment by becoming a monk and observing the rule of his order, so they had sought it by the discipline of the Holy Club and the renunciation involved in going to Georgia. (3) Then from the Moravians, especially Peter Böhler, and from Luther himself, they learned that the holiness and love which they sought was not to be found by the way of their own "good works" but by faith in Christ alone; and in May, 1738, they took their first trembling but excited steps along that way.(4) "But still holiness was their point." The goal they had set themselves long before remained still their goal. The way of faith must lead to love filling the heart and governing the life, or it was no true faith. "Faith working by love" was for them the sum and substance of Christianity and, indeed, of all true religion.[23]

It is true that the Wesleys were interested in "feeling" and "experience"; but the experience with which they were concerned was that of living faith in Christ, and what they wanted to "feel" was the fruit of that faith—love, peace, and joy, but above all, love. At Pentecost, 1738, they began to enter into this experience, taking, as we have said, "their first trembling but excited steps" along the way of faith. But this was only the beginning for them, and for days, weeks, and even months afterwards, they were beset by recurrent doubts and uncertainties, and had to wrestle with very contrary feelings. The following extracts from their writings reveal a continual struggle for faith and the gradual triumph of faith over feeling.

Charles Wesley's Experience.[24]

[*Evening of May 21*] . . . I now found myself at peace with God, and rejoiced in hope of loving Christ. My temper for the rest of the day was mistrust of my own great, but before unknown, weakness. I saw that by faith I stood; by the continual support of faith, which kept me from falling, though of myself I was ever sinking into sin.

Mon., May 22. Under [Christ's] protection I waked next morning, and rejoiced in reading the 107th Psalm, so nobly describing what God had done for my soul. Today I saw him chiefly as my King, and found him in his power: but saw little of the love of Christ crucified, or of my sins past; though more, I humbly hope, of my own weakness and his strength. I had many evil thoughts darted into my mind, but I rejected them immediately (yet not I).

Tue., May 23. I waked under the protection of Christ, and gave myself up, soul and body to him. At nine I began an hymn upon my conversion, but was persuaded to break off, for fear of pride. Mr. Bray coming, encouraged me to proceed in spite of Satan. I prayed Christ to stand by me, and finished the hymn.

Wed., May 24. Being to receive the sacrament today, I was assaulted by the fear of my old accustomed deadness; but soon recovered my confidence in Christ, that he would give me so much sense of his love now, as he saw good for me. I received [the sacrament] without any sensible devotion.

At eight [in the evening] I prayed by myself for love; with some feeling, and assurance of feeling more. Towards ten, my brother was brought in triumph by a troop of our friends, and declared "I believe." We sang the hymn with great joy, and parted with prayer. At midnight I gave myself up to Christ; assured I was safe, sleeping or waking.

Thur., May 25. I commended myself to Christ, my Prophet, Priest, and King. Before communicating, I left it to Christ, whether or in what measure he would please to manifest himself to me in this breaking of bread. I had no particular attention to the prayers. . . . At the same time, I felt great peace and joy; and assurance of feeling more, when it is best.

Soon after I was a little cast down, by feeling some temptation, and foreseeing more; but God lifted me up by his word: "Fear not: for I have redeemed thee, I have called thee by thy name; thou art mine. When thou passest through the waters, I will be with thee. . . . "; (Isa. 43:1f.). This promise was fulfilled in me when under frequent motions of sin I looked up to Christ, and found them beaten down continually.

Fri., May 26. . . . I dined with great liberty of spirit, being amazed to find my old enemy, intemperance, so suddenly subdued, that I have almost forgot I was ever in bondage to him. In the evening I broke through my own great unwillingness, and at last preached faith in Christ to an accidental visitant.

Sat., May 27. I felt a motion of anger, from a trifling disappointment; but it was no sooner felt than conquered. I received the sacrament: still no sensible love; but comfort.

Trinity Sunday, May 28. I rose in great heaviness, which neither private nor joint prayer could remove. At last I betook myself to intercession for my relations, and was greatly helped and enlarged herein; particularly in prayer for a most profligate sinner. I spent the morning with James Hutton, in prayer, and singing and rejoicing.

Thur., June 1. I was troubled today that I could not pray, being utterly dead at the sacrament.

Fri., June 2. I was still unable to pray; still dead in communicating; full of a cowardly desire of death.

Sat., June 3. My deadness continued, and the next day increased. I rose exceeding heavy and averse to prayer; so that I almost resolved not to go to church. When I did go, the prayers and sacrament were exceeding grievous to me; and I could not help asking myself, "Where is the difference between what I am now, and what I was before believing?" I immediately answered, "That the darkness was not like the former darkness, because I was satisfied there was no guilt in it; because I was assured it would be dispersed; and because, though I could not find I loved God, or feel that he loved me, yet I did and would believe he loved me notwithstanding."

In the evening Mr. Brown, Holland, and others called. I was very averse to coming among them, but forced myself to it, and spent two or three hours in singing, reading, and prayer. This exercise a little revived me; and I found myself much assisted to pray.

We asked particularly that, if it was the will of God, some one might now receive the atonement. While I was yet speaking the words, Mr. Brown found power to believe. He rose and told me my prayer was heard, and answered in him. We were all full of joy and thanksgiving. Before we parted,

I prayed with Mr. Brown, and praised God, to the great confirmation of my faith. The weight was quite taken off. I found power to pray with great earnestness, and rejoiced in my trials having continued so long, to show me that it is then the best time to labour for our neighbour, when we are cast down, and most unable to help ourselves.

Tue., June 6. In the evening I read Luther, as usual, to a large company of our friends. Mr. Burton was greatly affected. My inward temptations are, in a manner, uninterrupted. I never knew the energy of sin, till now that I experience the superior strength of Christ.

Wed., June 7. I found myself this morning under my [heavenly] Father's protection; and reading Matt. 7, "Ask and ye shall receive," I asked some sense of his love in the sacrament. It was there given me to believe assuredly that God loved me, even when I could have no sense of it. Some imperfect perception of his love I had, and was strengthened to hope against hope, after communicating.

Thur., June 8. . . . At three I took coach for Blendon, with Mr. Bray; and had much talk with a lady about the fall, and faith in Christ. She openly maintained the merit of good works. I would all who oppose the righteousness of faith were so ingenuous: then would they no longer seek it as it were by the works of the law.

Sun., June 11. . . . After prayers we joined in intercession for Mr. and Mrs. Delamotte; then for poor Hetty. I received much comfort in reading Luther.

[After church, we] joined in prayer for a poor woman in despair, one Mrs. Searl, whom Satan had bound these many years. I saw her pass by in the morning, and was touched with a sense of her misery. After pleading his promise of being with us to the end of the world, we went down to her in the name of Jesus. I asked her whether she thought God was love; and not anger, as Satan would persuade her. Then I preached the gospel, which she received with all imaginable eagerness. When we had for some time continued together in prayer, she rose up another creature, strongly and explicitly declaring her faith in the blood of Christ, and full persuasion that she was accepted in the Beloved. Hetty then declared that she could not but believe that Christ died for her, even for her. We gave thanks for both, with much exultation and triumph.

Wed., June 14. . . . Poor Hetty was tempted to imagine she did not believe, because she had not been affected exactly in the same manner with others. We used a prayer for her, and parted.

Thur., June 22. I comforted Hetty, under a strong temptation because she was not in all points affected like other believers, especially the poor; who have generally a much larger degree of confidence than the rich and learned.

Mon., July 10. At Mr. Sparks's request, I went with him, Mr. Bray, and Mr. Burnham, to Newgate; and preached to the ten malefactors under sentence of death; but with a heavy heart. My old prejudices against the possibility of a death-bed repentance still hung upon me; and I could hardly hope there was mercy for those whose time was so short. But in the midst of my languid discourse, a sudden spirit of faith came upon me, and I promised them all pardon in the name of Jesus Christ, if they would then, as at the last hour, repent and believe the gospel. Nay, I did believe they would accept of the proffered mercy, and could not help telling them, "I had no doubt but God would give me every soul of them."

Wed., July 12. I preached at Newgate to the condemned felons, and visited one of them in his cell, sick of a fever; a poor Black that had robbed his master. I told him of One who came down from heaven to save lost sinners, and him in particular; described the sufferings of the Son of God, his sorrows, agony, and death. He listened with all the signs of eager astonishment; the tears trickled down his cheeks while he cried, "What! was it for me? Did God suffer all this for so poor a creature as me?" I left him waiting for the salvation of God.

Sat., July 15. I preached there again with an enlarged heart; and rejoiced with my poor happy Black; who now *believes* the Son of God loved him, and gave himself for him.

Tue., July 18. . . . At night I was locked with Bray in one of the cells. We wrestled in mighty prayer. All the criminals were present; and all delightfully cheerful. Joy was visible in all their faces. We sang:

Behold the Saviour of mankind,
Nailed to the shameful tree!
How vast the love that him inclined
To bleed and die for thee![25]

Wed., July 19. . . . At half-hour past nine their irons were knocked off, and their hands tied. I went in a coach with Sparks, Washington, and a friend of Newington's. By half-hour past ten we came to Tyburn, waited till eleven: then were brought the children appointed to die. I got upon the cart with Sparks and Broughton. I prayed first, then Sparks and Broughton. We had prayed before that our Lord would show there was a power superior to the fear of death. They were all cheerful; full of comfort, peace, and triumph; assuredly persuaded Christ had died for them, and waited to receive them into paradise.

The Black had spied me coming out of the coach, and saluted me with his looks. As often as his eyes met mine, he smiled with the most composed, delightful countenance I ever saw. Read caught hold of my hand in a transport of joy. Newington seemed perfectly pleased. Hudson declared he was never better, or more at ease, in mind and body. None showed any natural terror of death: no fear, or crying, or tears. All expressed their desire of our following them to paradise. I never saw such calm triumph, such incredible indifference to dying. We sang several hymns; particularly,

> Behold the Saviour of mankind,
> Nailed to the shameful tree;

and the hymn entitled "Faith in Christ," which concludes:

> A guilty, weak, and helpless worm,
> Into thy hands I fall:
> Be thou my life, my righteousness,
> My Jesus, and my all.[26]

We prayed him, in earnest faith, to receive their spirits. I could do nothing but rejoice: kissed Newington and Hudson; took leave of each in particular. Mr. Broughton bade them not be surprised when the cart should draw away. They cheerfully replied they should not; expressed some concern how we should get back to our coach. We left them going to meet their Lord, ready for the Bridegroom. When the cart drew off, not one stirred or struggled for life, but meekly gave up their spirits. Exactly at twelve they were turned off. I spoke a few suitable words to the crowd; and returned, full of peace and confidence in our friends' happiness. That hour under the gallows was the most blessed hour of my life.

> O the goodness of God,
> Employing a clod
> His tribute of glory to raise!
> His standard to bear,
> And with triumph declare
> His unspeakable riches of grace.
>
> All honour and praise
> To the Father of grace,
> To the Spirit and Son I return!
> The business pursue
> He hath made me to do,
> And rejoice that I ever was born.
>
> In a rapture of joy
> My life I employ,
> The God of my life to proclaim;
> 'Tis worth living for this,
> To administer bliss
> And salvation in Jesus' name.

My remnant of days
I spend in his praise.
Who died the whole world to redeem:
Be they many or few.
My days are his due.
And they all are devoted to him.[27]

John Wesley's Experience.[28]

[*Evening of May 24*]. . . . It was not long before the enemy suggested, "This cannot be faith; for where is thy joy?" Then was I taught that peace and victory over sin are essential to faith in the Captain of our salvation; but that, as to the transports of joy that usually attend the beginning of it, especially in those who have mourned deeply, God sometimes giveth, sometimes withholdeth them, according to the counsels of his own will.

Thur., May 25. The moment I awaked, "Jesus, Master," was in my heart and in my mouth; and I found all my strength lay in keeping my eye fixed upon him, and my soul waiting on him continually. . . . Yet the enemy injected a fear, "If thou dost believe, why is there not a more sensible [perceptible] change?" I answered (yet not I), "That I know not. But this I know, I have now 'peace with God.' And I sin not today, and Jesus my Master has forbid me to take thought for the morrow."

"But is not any sort of fear," continued the tempter, "a proof that thou dost not believe?" I desired my Master to answer for me, and opened his Book upon those words of St. Paul, "Without were fightings, within were fears." Then, inferred I, well may fears be within me; but I must go on, and tread them under my feet.

Mon., May 29. I set out for Dummer with Mr. Wolf, one of the first-fruits of Peter Böhler's ministry in England. I was much strengthened by the grace of God in him. Yet was his state so far above mine, that I was often tempted to doubt whether we had one faith. But without much reasoning about it, I held here: "Though his be strong and mine weak, yet that God hath given some degree of faith even to me, I know by its fruits. For I have constant peace; not one uneasy thought. And I have freedom from sin; not one unholy desire."

Sun., June 4. Was indeed a feast-day. For from the time of my rising till past one in the afternoon, I was praying, reading the Scriptures, singing praise, or calling sinners to repentance. All these days I scarce remember to have opened the New Testament, but upon some "great and precious promise." And I saw more than ever that the gospel is in truth but one great promise, from the beginning of it to the end.

Tue., June 6. I had still more comfort, and peace, and joy; on which I fear I began to presume. For in the evening I received a letter from Oxford, which threw me into much perplexity. It was asserted therein, "That no doubting could consist with the least degree of true faith; that whoever at any time felt any doubt or fear was not weak in faith, but had no faith at all. . . ."

Begging of God to direct me, I opened my Testament on I Cor. 3:1ff., where St. Paul speaks of those whom he terms "babes in Christ," who were "not able to bear strong meat," nay (in a sense) "carnal"; to whom nevertheless he says, "Ye are God's building, ye are the temple of God." Surely, then, these men had some degree of faith; though it is plain, their faith was but weak.

Wed., June 7. I determined, if God should permit, to retire for a time into Germany. I had fully proposed, before I left Georgia, so to do, if it should please God to bring me back to Europe. And now I clearly saw the time was come. My weak mind could not bear to be thus sawn asunder. And I hoped the conversing with these holy men the Moravians, at Herrnhut, who were themselves living witnesses of the full power of faith, and yet able to bear with those that are weak, would be a means under God of so establishing my soul, that I might go on from faith to faith, and "from strength to strength."[29]

[Before leaving for Germany Wesley preached the University Sermon at Oxford on the afternoon of Sunday, June 11. This was the sermon on Salvation by Faith, which afterwards became the first of the Standard Sermons. Not a mean achievement for one who at the time was so "weak in faith"!]

Sun., Sept. 17. I began again to declare in my own country the glad tidings of salvation, preaching three times, and afterwards expounding the Holy Scripture to a large company in the Minories. On *Monday* I rejoiced to meet with our little society, which now consisted of thirty-two persons. The next day I went to the condemned felons in Newgate, and offered them free salvation.

Mon., Oct. 9. I set out for Oxford. In walking I read the truly surprising narrative of the conversions lately wrought in and about the town of Northampton, in New England [under the ministry of Jonathan Edwards]. Surely "this is the Lord's doing, and it is marvellous in our eyes." An extract from this I wrote to a friend, concerning the state of those who are "weak in faith." His answer, which I received at Oxford on *Saturday* the 14th., threw me into great perplexity. . . .

Sun., Oct. 29. . . . In the evening, being troubled at what some said of "the kingdom of God within us," and doubtful of my own state, I called upon God, and received this answer from his word: "He himself also waited for the kingdom of God" [Luke 23:51]. "But should not I wait in silence and retirement?" was the thought that immediately struck into my mind. I opened my Testament again, on those words, "Seest thou not how faith wrought together with his works? And by works was faith made perfect" [James 2:22].[30]

[*Mon., Oct. 30. John wrote in a letter to his brother Samuel:*] By a Christian I mean one who so believes in Christ as that sin hath no more dominion over him; and in this obvious sense of the word I was not a Christian till May the 24th last past. For till then sin had the dominion over me, although I fought with it continually; but surely then, from that time to this it hath not, such is the free grace of God in Christ.

If you ask by what means I am made free (though not perfect, neither infallibly sure of my perseverance), I answer, by faith in Christ; by such a sort or degree of faith as I had not till that day. My desire of this faith I knew long before, though not so clearly till Sunday, January the 8th last.[31]. . . . Some measure of this faith, which bringeth salvation or victory over sin, and which implies peace and trust in God through Christ, I now enjoy by his free mercy; though in very deed it is in me but as a grain of mustard seed: for the πληοφπρία πίστεως—the seal of the Spirit, the love of God shed abroad in my heart, and producing joy in the Holy Ghost—this witness of the Spirit I have not; but I patiently wait for it. And having seen and spoken with a cloud of witnesses abroad as well as in my own country, I cannot doubt but that believers who wait and pray for it will find these scriptures fulfilled in themselves. My hope is that they will be fulfilled in me. I build on Christ, the Rock of Ages; on his sure mercies described in his Word; and on his promises, all which I know are yea and amen. Those who have not yet received joy in the Holy Ghost, the love of God, and the plerophory of faith (any or all of which I take to be the witness of the Spirit with our spirit that we are the sons of God), I believe to be Christians in that imperfect sense wherein I may call myself such; and I exhort them to pray that God would give them also "to rejoice in the hope of the glory of God," and to feel "his love shed abroad in their hearts by the Holy Ghost which is given unto them."[32]

Thur., Jan. 4, 1739—One who had had the form of godliness many years wrote the following reflections:

My friends affirm that I am mad, because I said I was not a Christian a year ago. I affirm I am not a Christian now. Indeed, what I might have been I know not, had I been faithful to the grace then given, when, expecting nothing less, I received such a sense of the forgiveness of my sins as till then I never knew. But that I am not a Christian at this day I as assuredly know as that Jesus is the Christ.

For a Christian is one who has the fruits of the Spirit of Christ, which (to mention no more) are love, peace, joy. But these I have not. I have not any love of God. I do not love either the Father or the Son. Do you ask, how do I know whether I love God? I answer by another question, "How do you know whether you love me?" Why, as you know whether you are hot or cold. You *feel* this moment that you do or do not love me. And I *feel* this moment I do not love God; which therefore I *know* because I *feel* it. There is no word more proper, more clear, or more strong.

Wed., Jan. 10. I preached at Basingshaw church *Saturday* the 13th. I expounded to a large company at Beech Lane. *Sunday* the 14th, after preaching at Islington, I expounded twice at Mr. Sims's in the Minories.

Sun., Feb. 4. I preached at St. Giles's on "Whosoever believeth on Me, out of his belly shall flow rivers of living water." How was the power of God present with us! I am content to preach here no more.[33]

Fri., Mar. 2. It was the advice of all our brethren that I should spend a few days at Oxford, whither I accordingly went on *Saturday* the 3rd. A few names I found here also who had not denied the faith, neither been ashamed of their Lord, even in the midst of a perverse generation. And every day we were together we had convincing proof, such as it had not before entered into our hearts to conceive, that "He is able to save unto the uttermost all that come to God through him."

Thursday the 15th. I set out early in the morning, and in the afternoon came to London. During my stay here. . . . I received, after several others, a letter from Mr. Whitefield, and another from Mr. Seward, entreating me in the most pressing manner to come to Bristol without delay. This I was not at all forward to do.

Sat., Mar. 31. In the evening I reached Bristol, and met Mr. Whitefield there. I could scarce reconcile myself at first to this strange way of preaching in the fields, of which he set me an example on Sunday; having been all my life (until very lately) so tenacious of every point relating to decency and order, that I should have thought the saving of souls almost a sin if it had not been done in a church.

Sun., Apr. 1. In the evening I began expounding our Lord's Sermon on the Mount (one pretty remarkable example of field-preaching, though I suppose there were churches at that time also) to a little society which was accustomed to meet once or twice a week in Nicholas Street.

Mon., Apr. 2. At four in the afternoon I submitted to be more vile, and proclaimed in the highways the glad tidings of salvation, speaking from a little eminence in a ground adjoining to the city, to about three thousand people. The scripture on which I spoke was this (is it possible any one should be ignorant that it is fulfilled in every true minister of Christ?), "The Spirit of the Lord is upon me, because he hath anointed me to preach the gospel to the poor. He hath sent me to heal the broken-hearted; to preach deliverance to the captives, and recovery of sight to the blind; to set at liberty them that are bruised, to proclaim the acceptable year of the Lord."[34]

Shall I, for fear of feeble man,
The Spirit's course in me restrain?
Or, undismayed, in deed and word
Be a true witness for my Lord?

Saviour of men, thy searching eye
Doth all my inmost thoughts descry;
Doth aught on earth my wishes raise,
Or the world's pleasures or its praise?

The love of Christ doth me constrain
To seek the wandering souls of men;
With cries, entreaties, tears, to save,
To snatch them from the gaping grave.

My life, my blood, I here present,
If for thy truth they may be spent:
Fulfil thy sovereign counsel, Lord;
Thy will be done, thy name adored.

Give me thy strength, O God of power;
Then, let winds blow or thunders roar,
Thy faithful witness will I be:
'Tis fixed; I can do all through thee![35]

More than a decade later, John Wesley wrote in a reply to a critic who had commented adversely on several passages in his *Journal:*

> [You quote me as saying:] ". . . . I cannot find in myself the love of God or of Christ. Hence my deadness and wanderings in public prayer. Hence it is that even in the Holy Communion I have rarely any more than a cold attention. Hence, when I hear of the highest instance of God's love, my heart is still senseless and unaffected. Yea, at this moment (October 14, 1738) I feel no more love to him than one I had never heard of."
>
> To any who knew something of inward religion I should have observed that this is what serious divines mean by desertion. But all expressions of this kind are jargon to you. So, allowing it to be whatever you please, I ask only, Do you know how long I continued in this state? How many years, months, weeks, or days? If not, how can you infer what my state of mind is now from what it was above eleven years ago?
>
> Sir, I do not tell you or any man else that "I cannot now find the love of God in myself"; or that now, in the year 1751, I rarely feel more than a cold attention in the Holy Communion: so that your whole argument built upon this supposition falls to the ground at once.[36]

Yet nearly a quarter of a century after this, he wrote to a certain correspondent: "I feel more want of heat than light. I value light; but it is nothing compared to love."[37] And after another decade he wrote yet again:

I do not remember to have heard or read anything like my own experience. Almost ever since I can remember, I have been led in a peculiar way. I go on in an even line, being very little raised at one time or depressed at another. Count Zinzendorf observes there are three different ways wherein it pleases God to lead his people: some are guided in almost every instance by apposite texts of Scripture; others see a clear and plain reason for everything they are to do; and yet others are led not so much by Scripture or reason as by particular impressions. I am very rarely led by impressions, but generally by reason and by Scripture. I see abundantly more than I feel. I want to feel more love and zeal for God.[38]

John Wesley's heart may have been "strangely warmed" at Aldersgate, but it was only warm, not hot, and it was strange for it even to be warm. John seems clearly never to have experienced the intensity of feeling that he knew thousands of others did; and there is a remarkable letter to his brother Charles, written in 1766, in which he declares he never had any love for God, nor any real faith. "And yet," he says:

I dare not preach otherwise than I do, either concerning faith or love, or justification, or perfection. And yet I find rather an increase than a decrease of zeal for the whole work of God and every part of it. I am Φερόμενος [borne along], I know not how, that I can't stand still. I want all the world to come to ὁὺ οὐκ οἶδα [Him whom I do not know]. Neither am I impelled to this by fear of any kind. I have no more fear than love. Or if I have [[any fear, it is not that of falling]] into hell but of falling into nothing.[39]

But the man who could write thus could also translate Johann Andreas Rothe's great hymn, *"Ich habe nun den Grund gefunden,"* and could put into his translation the depth of feeling that the following verses express:

O Love, thou bottomless abyss,
  My sins are swallowed up in thee!
Covered is my unrighteousness,
  Nor spot of guilt remains on me,
While Jesus blood through earth and skies
Mercy, free, boundless mercy! cries.

With faith I plunge me in this sea,
  Here is my hope, my joy, my rest;
Hither, when hell assails, I flee,
  I look into my Saviour's breast:

Away, sad doubt and anxious fear!
Mercy is all that's written there.

Though waves and storms go o'er my head,
  Though strength, and health, and friends be gone,
Though joys be withered all and dead,
  Though every comfort be withdrawn,
On this my steadfast soul relies—
Father, thy mercy never dies.

Fixed on this ground will I remain,
  Though my heart fail and flesh decay;
This anchor shall my soul sustain,
  When earth's foundations melt away:
Mercy's full power I then shall prove,
Loved with an everlasting love.[40]

II

Fulfilment of a Mission

"METHODISM SO CALLED"

When John Wesley traveled up and down the United Kingdom for fifty years, covering six thousand miles a year on horseback or by coach, holding conferences, forming societies, and preaching in all some forty thousand sermons, he had no intention of founding a new church, still less a sect. The very idea was repugnant to him, and it was even more repugnant to Charles. They were clergymen of the Church of England, and most of those working with them, as John tells us in his *Short History of Methodism* [ca. 1764], were "Church of England men." They loved the doctrine, the liturgy, and the discipline of the Church of England and did not willingly vary from it in any instance.[1] Nevertheless, they were called (though not by their own choice) "Methodists," and the movement they led possessed distinct characteristics of its own—largely shaped by John Wesley. It could be argued, indeed, that Wesley himself succeeded in making the People called Methodists into a distinct and eventually separate body.

The reasons for this were not of course doctrinal. For Methodism, as Wesley again and again insisted, was nothing else but "the religion of the Bible, the Primitive Church, and the Church of England,"[2] and with the doctrinal standards of the Church of England they had no quarrel. Their teaching was wholly in harmony with that of the Articles, the Homilies, and the Book of Common Prayer. It was in fact the common doctrine of Christendom, presented with certain particular emphases that were characteristically but by no means exclusively Methodist. What became chiefly important for the distinct and separate life of Methodism was Wesley's organization of his followers into societies, which were linked together in a strongly unified "Connexion." This was very necessary if the work of the Methodist Revival was not to be largely dissipated, but it was almost inevitable that it should result in the creation of the Methodist Church. No doubt, if the Church of England had possessed more imagination, not to mention Christian insight and charity, Methodism (at least in

Britain) might have developed into an Order within that Church; but in the circumstances that could not be.

How impossible it was can be illustrated from a letter written by Wesley in the last year of his life to the Bishop of Lincoln:

> The Methodists in general, my Lord, are members of the Church of England. They hold all her doctrines, attend her service, and partake of her sacraments. They do not willingly do harm to anyone, but do what good they can to all. To encourage each other herein they frequently spend an hour together in prayer and mutual exhortation. Permit me then to ask, *Cui bono,* "for what reasonable end," would your Lordship drive these people out of the Church? Are they not as quiet, as inoffensive, nay as pious, as any of their neighbours—except perhaps here and there an hairbrained man who knows not what he is about? Do you ask, "Who drives them out of the Church?" Your Lordship does; and that in the most cruel manner—yea, and the most disingenuous manner. They desire a licence to worship God after their own conscience. Your Lordship refuses it, and then punishes them for not having a licence! So your Lordship leaves them only this alternative, "Leave the Church or starve." And is it a Christian, yea a Protestant bishop, that so persecutes his own flock? I say, *persecutes;* for it is persecution to all intents and purposes. You do not burn them indeed, but you starve them. And how small is the difference! And your Lordship does this under colour of a vile, execrable law, not a whit better than that *de haeretico comburendo* [concerning the burning of heretics]. So persecution, which is banished out of France, is again countenanced in England! O my Lord, for God's sake, for Christ's sake, for pity's sake, suffer the poor people to enjoy their religious as well as civil liberty![3]

At the same time, it cannot be overlooked that Wesley instituted a discipline for both the preachers and the members of the Methodist Societies which was not that of the Church of England and over which the authorities of that Church had no control. He gave them Lovefeasts and Watchnight Services and Tickets of Membership, following precedents he found in the Early Church; and he gave them a Covenant Service that was all their own. He revised the Articles of Religion and the Book of Common Prayer for the Methodists in America *(The Sunday Service of the Methodists),* and what was still more fateful, he ordained preachers to minister to them—an action that had repercussions also in Britain. He also published a series of hymn books, notably one entitled *A Collection of Hymns for the Use of the People Called Methodists* (1780), which, with their successors, became the Prayer book and liturgy of Methodism, nourishing the souls both of the individual Christian and the Society. With all this, it was virtually impossible that the People called Methodists should not come to feel themselves a distinct if not separate body, especially when they met with all kinds of unfriendliness from many of the bishops and clergy. There were in consequence periodic agitations among them in favour of separation from the Church; and although Wesley successfully resisted these, so that British Methodism did not become explicitly a separate denomination till long after his death, he was forced towards the end of his life to bow to the logic of events and assist in the setting up of The Methodist Church in America.

Nevertheless, in all that he did, Wesley had, in his own words, only "one point in view—to promote, so far as I am able, vital, practical religion; and by the grace of God to beget, preserve, and increase the life of God in the souls of men."[4] "It is not our care, endeavour, or desire, to proselyte any from one man to another; or from one church (so called), from one congregation or society, to another—we would not move a finger to do this, to make ten thousand such proselytes—but from darkness to light, from Belial to Christ, from the power of Satan to God. Our one aim is to proselyte sinners to repentance, the servants of the devil to serve the living and true God."[5] "We look upon ourselves, not as the authors or ringleaders of a particular sect or party (it is the farthest thing from our thoughts), but as messengers of God to those who are Christians in name, but Heathens in heart and life, to call them back to that from which they are fallen, to real, genuine Christianity. We are therefore debtors to all these, of whatever opinion or denomination; and are consequently to do all that in us lies, to please all for their good to edification. We look upon the Methodists (so called) in general, not as any particular party (this would exceedingly obstruct the grand design for which we conceive God has raised them up), but as living witnesses, in and to every party, of that Christianity which we preach, which is hereby demonstrated to be a real thing, and visibly held out to all the world."[6]

The majority of the Methodists, it is true, were Anglicans; but it was a peculiar glory of Methodism, in Wesley's view, that while it was a religious society within the Church of England, it was one to which members of any church might belong, the only condition of membership being "a real desire to save their soul."[7] "By Methodists," he said, "I mean a people who profess to pursue (in whatsoever measure they have attained) holiness of heart and life, inward and outward conformity in all things to the revealed will of God; who place religion in a uniform resemblance of the great object of it; in a steady imitation of Him they worship, in all his imitable perfections; more particularly, in justice, mercy, and truth, or universal love filling the heart and governing the life."[8] In order to pursue such an end, it was not necessary that men should renounce their existing ecclesiastical allegiance. And just as Wesley always exhorted the Methodist Anglicans to be loyal to their own Church, so he encouraged the Methodist Presbyterians, Baptists, Congregationalists, and Quakers to do the same. Indeed, he regarded it as highly undesirable that they should do anything else, for Methodism could fulfil its true function only as an interdenominational society, not as a separate denomination. "The Methodists," he insisted, "are to spread life among all denominations; which they will do till they form a separate sect."[9]

"But," said some of his critics, "you form a Church within a Church, whose members in South Britain profess to belong to the Church of England, and those in North Britain to the Church of Scotland; while yet they are inspected and governed by Teachers who are sent, continued, or removed, by Mr. W." To which Wesley replied: "All this is in a certain sense very true. But let us see what it amounts to. 'You form a Church within a Church'; that is, you raise up and join together witnesses of real Christianity, not among Mahometans and Pagans, but within a Church by law established. Certainly so. And that Church, if she knew her own interest, would see she is much obliged to us for so doing."[10] Not, however, that Wesley ever maintained that the members of his Methodist Societies were the only "witnesses of real Christianity," nor, indeed, that they could alone be called Methodists. "There are many thousand Methodists in Great Britain and Ireland," he wrote to a correspondent in Sweden in 1769, "which are not formed into Societies. Indeed, none are but those (or rather a part of those) who are under the care of Mr. Wesley. These at present contain a little less than thirty thousand persons."[11] In other words, one could be a Methodist in John Wesley's understanding of the term, not only without leaving one's own denomination, but without becoming a member of the Methodist Society. All that was necessary was that one should be seriously pursuing "holiness in heart and life."

Wesley was, however, early accused of breaches of ecclesiastical order on account of the methods he employed: his open-air preaching, his permitting of laymen to preach, his use of extempore prayer, and his working in other men's parishes. But to all such charges he had a ready answer.

"You ask, 'How is it that I assemble Christians, who are none of my charge, to sing psalms and pray and hear the Scriptures expounded?' and think it hard to justify doing this in other men's parishes, upon catholic principles. Permit me to speak plainly. If by catholic principles you mean any other than scriptural, they weigh nothing with me. I allow no other rule, whether of faith or practice, than the Holy Scriptures; but on scriptural principles I do not think it hard to justify whatever I do. God in Scripture commands me, according to my power, to instruct the ignorant, reform the wicked, confirm the virtuous. Man forbids me to do this in another's parish: that is, in effect, to do it at all; seeing I have now no parish of my own, nor probably ever shall. Whom, then, shall I hear, God or man? 'If it be just to obey man rather than God, judge you. A dispensation of the gospel is committed to me; and woe is me if I preach not the gospel.' Suffer me now to tell you my principles in this matter. I look upon all the world as my parish; thus far, I mean, that in whatever part of it I am I judge it meet, right and my bounden duty, to declare unto all that are willing to hear, the glad tidings of salvation. This is the work which I know God has called me to; and sure I am that his blessing attends it."[12]

"It is true in some things we vary from the rules of our Church; but no further than we apprehend is our bounden duty. It is upon a full conviction of this that we. . . permit laymen whom God has called to preach. I say *permit,* because we ourselves have hitherto viewed it in no other light. It is not clear to us that presbyters so circumstanced as we are may *appoint* or *ordain* others, but it is that we may *direct* as well as *suffer* them to do what we conceive they are *moved* to *by the Holy Ghost.* It is true that in ordinary cases both an *inward* and an *outward* call are requisite. But we apprehend there is something far from *ordinary* in the present case. And upon the calmest view of things, we think they who are only called of God and not of man have *more* right to preach than they who are only called of man and not of God. Now, that many of the clergy, though called of man, are not called of God to preach his gospel is undeniable, (1) because they themselves utterly disclaim, nay, ridicule, the inward call; (2) because they do not know what the gospel is, of consequence they do not and cannot preach it. Dear sir, coolly and impartially consider this, and you will see on which side the difficulty lies. I see those running whom God hath not sent, destroying their own souls and those that hear them. I see the blind leading the blind and both falling into the ditch. Unless I warn in all ways I can these perishing souls of their danger, am I clear of the blood of these men? Soul-damning clergymen lay me under more difficulties than soul-saving laymen."[13]

As to attacks on his open-air preaching and use of extempore prayer, Wesley writes: "I have often replied: (1) It were better for me to die than not to preach the gospel of Christ; yea and in the fields, either where I may not preach in the church or where the church will not contain the congregation. (2) That I use the Service of the Church every Lord's Day, and it has never yet appeared to me that any rule of the Church forbids my using extemporary prayer on other occasions." He then proceeds:

But methinks I would go deeper. I would inquire, what is the end of all ecclesiastical order? Is it not to bring souls from the power of Satan to God, and to build them up in his fear and love? Order, then, is so far valuable as it answers these ends; and if it answers them not, it is nothing worth. Now I would fain know, where has order answered these ends? Not in any place where I have been—not among the tinners in Cornwall, the keelmen at Newcastle, the colliers in Kingswood or Staffordshire; not among the drunkards, swearers, Sabbath-breakers of Moorfields, or the harlots of Drury Lane. They could not be built up in the fear and love of God while they were open, barefaced servants of the devil; and such they continued, notwithstanding the most orderly preaching both in St. Luke's and St. Giles's Church. One reason whereof was, they never came near the church, nor had any desire or design to do so, till, by what you term 'breach of order' they were brought to fear God, to love him, and to keep his commandments. It was not, therefore, so much the want of order as of the knowledge and love of God which kept those poor souls for so many years in open bondage to an hard master. And indeed, wherever the knowledge and love of God are, true order will not be wanting. But the most apostolical order, where these are not, is less than nothing and vanity."[14]

It is true, Wesley admits, "I still believe 'the Episcopal form of Church government to be both scriptural and apostolical': I mean, well agreeing with the practice and writings of the Apostles. But that it is prescribed in Scripture I do not believe. This opinion (which I once heartily espoused) I have been heartily ashamed of ever since I read Dr. Stillingfleet's *Irenicon*. I think he has unanswerably proved that neither Christ nor his Apostles prescribed any particular form of Church government, and that the plea for the divine right of Episcopacy was never heard of in the primitive Church. But were it otherwise, I would still call these 'smaller points than the love of God and mankind.'"[15]

"OUR DOCTRINES"

Let us now turn to look at the characteristic teaching of the Wesleys and their Methodism. As we do so, it should of course be constantly borne in mind that this rests solidly upon the doctrinal heritage of the Christian centuries. The great and fundamental doctrines of the Trinity, the Incarnation, the Atonement, the Holy Spirit, and the Church are unquestioningly presupposed in all John Wesley's sermons, tracts, and treatises, and they are frequently celebrated in Charles Wesley's hymns. At the same time, there are other doctrines, corollaries of these, that are singled out for special emphasis and that must be regarded as of the very essence of Methodism. John Wesley often spoke of them as "our doctrines,"not as implying that they were in any way exclusively Methodist (for they were and are not), but that Methodists had a special responsibility for them.

Wesley produced no specific formulation of those doctrines, though he summarised them again and again in a variety of ways. The following, from a reply to misrepresentations of a critic in the public press, is an example:

> The fundamental doctrine of the people called Methodists is, Whosoever will be saved, before all things it is necessary that he hold the true faith—the faith which works by love; which, by means of the love of God and our neighbour, produces both inward and outward holiness. This faith is an evidence of things not seen; and he that thus believes is regenerate, or born of God; and he has the witness in himself (call it assurance or what you please): the Spirit itself witnesses with his spirit that he is a child of God. "From what scripture" every one of these propositions "is collected" any common Concordance will show. "This is the true portraiture of Methodism," so called. "A religion superior to this" (the love of God and man) none can "enjoy," either in time or in eternity.[16]

In what follows, however, we shall review Wesley's teaching in terms of a simple fourfold formula, which, although not Wesley's own, admirably represents his mind and is rather more comprehensive than any single statement of his. It is this: (1) All men need to be saved; (2) all men can be saved; (3) all men can know they are saved; (4) all men can be saved to the uttermost.

We shall also draw on Charles Wesley's hymns to illustrate aspects of this teaching, and to show what was perhaps the most effective single means the Wesleys devised for instilling it into their people. These hymns expound the great catholic doctrines of the faith and interpret evangelical experience; and so long as they were sung—together with some of Isaac Watts and Philip Doddrige—the Methodists could not have a bad theology, whatever they heard preached from the pulpit. In the Preface to *A Collection of Hymns for the Use of the People Called Methodists,* John Wesley describes the book as "a little body of experimental and practical divinity," and claims that it contains "all the important truths of our most holy religion, whether speculative or practical, . . . carefully ranged under proper heads, according to the experience of real Christians."[17] By contrast with modern hymn books, whose table of contents usually resembles that of a treatise on systematic theology, Wesley's arrangement is far more 'existential.' The Methodists learned their theology by singing it, and they sang it not only into their heads but their hearts.

(1) All men need to be saved.

Why do they? Because all men are sinners. All men are either self-indulgent sinners like the Prodigal Son, or self-righteous sinners like his Elder Brother, or else, like most of us, they are something of both. As St. Paul says, "All have sinned and fall short of the glory of God."

This doctrine was not popular in the eighteenth century—the Age of Enlightenment. The prevailing temper of the time was one of optimistic humanism, cheerful faith in the possibilities of man. All that men needed, it was generally believed, was more knowledge, more education, more enlightenment, and then their problems would be solved. Against this Wesley set the ancient Christian doctrine of "original sin."[18] Certainly he agreed that men need more education and enlightenment, but they need more than that. They need salvation, a deep and radical deliverance from sin—from their estrangement from God—and this is something they cannot get for themselves. They need to be saved, they need a Saviour. Even good men need him, as John and Charles Wesley themselves had found.

It is strange how latter-day Methodism seems often to have forgotten that good men need to be saved. The typical example of conversion has come to be that of the drunkard made sober, and it hardly appears that the sober man has anything to be saved from. Yet the founders of Methodism had never been drunkards, nor had they indulged in any other kind of reprehensible behaviour. They were not Prodigals; they were good men. They were in fact Christian Pharisees, as both of them confess:

> A goodly, formal saint
> I long appeared in sight,
> By self and nature taught to paint
> My tomb, my nature, white.
> The Pharisee within
> Still undisturbed remained,
> The strong man, armed with guilt of sin,
> Safe in his palace reigned.
>
> But O, the jealous God
> In my behalf came down;
> Jesus himself the stronger showed,
> And claimed me for his own;

My spirit he alarmed,
And brought into distress;
He shook and bound the strong man armed
In his self-righteousness.[19]

It is not surprising, then, that Wesley's hymn book opens with a section "Exhorting Sinners to Return to God," which includes among others the following:

Sinners, turn, why will ye die?
God, your Maker, asks you why?
God, who did your being give,
Made you with himself to live;
He the fatal cause demands,
Asks the work of his own hands,
Why, ye thankless creatures, why
Will ye cross his love, and die?[20]

This hymn, incidentally, also inculcates the doctrine of the Trinity, the second line of the second verse being "God, your Saviour, asks you why?" and of the third, "God, the Spirit, asks you why?" It then concludes with a verse too strong to be included in modern hymn books:

Dead, already dead within,
Spiritually dead in sin,
Dead to God while here you breathe,
Pant ye after second death?
Will you still in sin remain,
Greedy of eternal pain?
O ye dying sinners, why,
Why will you forever die?[21]

Then follows another, longer section, in which the strong reasons are set forth why sinners should return to God. It begins with hymns describing "The Pleasantness of Religion" and "The Goodness of God," then moves on to the awful solemnity of "Death," "Judgment," "Heaven," and "Hell." Interestingly, there is only one hymn on hell, and even those on death and judgment more often strike a note of confident hope and joyful expectation than of fear and gloom. The Wesleys knew well how to warn men of the peril in which sin and ungodliness involved them, but they also knew that merely to frighten them would not save them; they must be won by the love and mercy of God. Hence, while the first part of the hymn on hell begins:

Terrible thought! shall I alone,
Who may be saved—shall I—
Of all, alas! whom I have known,
Through sin for ever die?

the second part is in another key:

Ah, no! I still may turn and live,
For still his wrath delays;
He now vouchsafes a kind reprieve,
And offers me his grace.[22]

(2) All men can be saved.

How can they? Only one answer is possible: through Jesus Christ and his atoning work.

Jesus comes with all his grace,
Comes to save a fallen race;
Object of our glorious hope,
Jesus comes to lift us up![23]

Consequently, the exhortation to return to God becomes an invitation to come to Jesus, to respond to his love and grace.

To save what was lost, from heaven he came;
Come, sinners, and trust in Jesus's name;
He offers you pardon, he bids you be free:
If sin be your burden, O come unto me![24]

Ye thirsty for God, to Jesus give ear,
And take, through his blood, a power to draw near;
His kind invitation ye sinners embrace,
Accepting salvation, salvation by grace.[25]

But here again was a doctrine that ran counter to eighteenth-century sentiment, and that in two directions.

First, men under the influence of rationalism and Deism could make no sense of the Atonement because they had no sense of sin. They could see no need of a Mediator between man and God because they had no awareness of the tragic depth of man's estrangement from God.[26] Secondly, men of Calvinistic sympathies, although they accepted the Atonement, could not approve of Wesley's way of preaching it. With their doctrine of predestination, they held that

Christ did not die for all men but only for the elect, so that for the rest of men there was no possibility of salvation. By contrast, Wesley insisted that "God wills all men to be saved" and that Christ died for all so that all may come to him and be saved, if only they will.

> Father, whose everlasting love
> Thy only Son for sinners gave,
> Whose grace to *all* did freely move,
> And sent him down *the world* to save;
>
> Help us thy mercy to extol,
> Immense, unfathomed, *unconfined;*
> To praise the Lamb who died for *all,*
> The *general* Saviour of mankind.
>
> The *world* he suffered to redeem;
> For *all* he hath the atonement made;
> For *those that will not come to him,*
> The ransom of his life was paid.[27]

Wherever we find phrases like those here italicised in a Wesley hymn, we may suspect it was written with a consciously anti-Calvinist intent.

But how do we, how can we, respond to Wesley's invitation to "come to Christ"? Nowadays it is often suggested that there are many different ways, almost as many as there are different people. But Wesley knows of only one way, the way of repentance and faith. For however different from one another we human beings may be, we are all alike in this, that we are sinners in need of salvation. And we can find salvation only as we acknowledge and confess that we are sinners (which is repentance) and believe that Jesus Christ came into the world to save sinners, and therefore to save *us* (which is faith).

> He dies to atone for sins not his own;
> Your debt he hath paid, and your work he hath done.
> Ye all may receive the peace he did leave,
> Who made intercession: My Father, forgive!
>
> For you and for me he prayed on the tree;
> The prayer is accepted, the sinner is free.
> That sinner am I, who on Jesus rely,
> And come for the Pardon God cannot deny.
> My pardon I claim; for a sinner I am,
> A sinner believing in Jesus's name. . . .[28]

That is repentance and faith; that is the way of salvation.

Not that it is easy to repent and believe, even when we see that we need to and even when we want to. We are so apt to be sorry for ourselves rather than for our sins, repenting because they have found us out rather than because we ever committed them; and when we are truly penitent, we find it easier to believe that Christ is the Saviour of the world than that he is *ours*. Wesley therefore teaches us to pray for the gift of repentance and faith.

O that I could repent!
  O that I could believe!
Thou by thy voice the marble rent,
  The rock in sunder cleave!
  Thou by thy two-edged sword,
  My soul and spirit part,
Strike with the hammer of thy word,
  And break my stubborn heart!

Saviour, and Prince of peace,
  The double grace bestow;
Unloose the bands of wickedness,
  And let the captive go:
  Grant me my sins to feel,
  And then the load remove;
Wound, and pour in, my wounds to heal,
  The balm of pardoning love.[29]

When this happens and we do repent and believe, then we are saved—and we can know we are saved.

(3) All men can know they are saved.

Notice here that Wesley says "can" know, not that they "must" know. He does not hold that a man cannot be saved unless he knows, as if knowing and being sure of it were a condition of salvation. What he contends is that everyone who is saved *can* have knowledge of it, and it is desirable that he should. We have no right to say that a person who is not sure is therefore not saved, but we do have a right to tell him he can be sure and to urge and help him to find assurance.[30]

But what is it precisely that a man knows when he knows he is saved, and how does he know? First of all, he knows that he is "justified"; that is to say, he is pardoned and accepted by God, so that there is no estrangement between him and God any more. He knows that he has "received the adoption"; he is accepted by God as a child of God, and he knows God as his heavenly Father. He knows that he has been "born again"; he has started life afresh as a child of God by the power of the Spirit of God. For salvation means not only forgiveness, it means also the gift of the Holy Spirit. That is what a man knows, who knows that he is saved.

As to how he knows, the answer lies in the gift of the Spirit. "The Spirit himself bears witness with our spirit that we are children of God." It is by the Holy Spirit, the Spirit of God and of Christ, that we are enabled to pray to God just as Jesus did, saying "Abba, Father." And it is by the same Spirit we are enabled to live as children of God should, so that "the fruit of the Spirit" is seen in our lives: "love, joy, peace, patience, kindness, goodness, faithfulness, gentleness, self-control." Here, in the witness of the Spirit and the fruit of the Spirit, is the heart of the Wesleyan doctrine of "assurance."

> How can a sinner know
> His sins on earth forgiven?
> How can my gracious Saviour show
> My name inscribed in heaven?
>
> What we have felt and seen
> With confidence we tell,
> And publish to the sons of men
> The signs infallible.
>
> His Spirit to us he gave,
> And dwells in us we know;
> The witness in ourselves we have,
> And all its fruits we show.[31]

Is this an arrogant claim? There are those who say it is. They hold we have no right to be so cocksure; the most we have any right to is a "sober trust" that we "may" be saved; and to claim "assurance" is to be guilty of overweening self-confidence. (The eighteenth century accused the Methodists of "enthusiasm," religious fanaticism, because of it.) But this is a complete misunderstanding. Wesleyan assurance is as far as possible removed from *self*-confidence. It is the very opposite of *self*-confidence, for it is confidence in *God,* and in God alone. It is an assurance concerning God, who in Christ has shown himself a good and gracious Father to us and has given us the Spirit of sonship, of which the fruit can be seen in our lives. Furthermore, it is an assurance regarding our *present* standing with God, not an infallible guarantee of our future destiny. It is no more that than falling in love and getting married is a guarantee of a permanently happy marriage—though they would be strange lovers who were not firmly convinced that they were going to be "happy ever after."

From this assurance springs the joyfulness of all true Methodist piety, and the lyrical quality of countless Wesley hymns.

O what shall I do my Saviour to praise,
So faithful and true, so plenteous in grace,
So strong to deliver, so good to redeem
The weakest believer that hangs upon him.

How happy the man whose heart is set free,
The people that can be joyful in thee!
Their joy is to walk in the light of thy face,
And still they are talking of Jesus's grace.[32]

My God, I am thine;
What a comfort divine,
What a blessing to know that my Jesus
is mine!
In the heavenly Lamb
Thrice happy I am,
And my heart it doth dance at the sound
of his name.[33]

(4) All men can be saved to the uttermost.

The work of salvation is not completed with "conversion," that is, with justification, adoption, the new birth, or even with assurance. These things are only the beginning from which we must go on, Wesley insists, to "entire sanctification" or "Christian perfection."

Sanctification means being made holy, and holiness is in Wesley's view, as we have seen, nothing else but love. It is love for God with all our heart and mind and soul and strength, in response to the love he has shown to us in Christ; and it is love for our neighbour "as ourselves," so that we treat our neighbour in the way that God in Christ has treated us, showing to him the same Spirit of love. But this, of course, is something we cannot do of ourselves, in our own strength and by our own resources. It is God's work in us that we must seek to have him do. In the hymn book, therefore, Wesley includes a whole series of hymns under the heading "For Believers Seeking Full Redemption" (i.e., "Entire Sanctification"). Here are some examples:

Purge me from every evil blot;
My idols all be cast aside;
Cleanse me from every sinful thought,
From all the filth of self and pride.

Give me a new, a Perfect heart,
  From doubt, and fear, and sorrow free;
The mind which was in Christ impart,
  And let my spirit cleave to thee.[34]

What! never speak one evil word,
  Or rash, or idle, or unkind!
O how shall I, most gracious Lord,
  This mark of true perfection find?

Thy sinless mind in me reveal,
  Thy Spirit's plenitude impart;
And all my spotless life shall tell
  The abundance of a loving heart.[35]

I want thy life, thy purity,
  Thy righteousness brought in;
I ask, desire, and trust in thee,
  To be redeemed from sin.

Anger and sloth, desire and pride,
  This moment be subdued!
Be cast into the crimson tide
  Of my Redeemer's blood![36]

Sanctification is begun in us, Wesley teaches, as soon as ever we receive God's gift of pardon and the Holy Spirit. But it is only begun, and most of us have a long way to go before it is completed. Most of us, indeed, are unlikely to attain perfect holiness till we are on our death-beds, though many might attain it earlier, if only they were earnest enough in seeking it. In the meantime, however, the process of being made holy involves us in conflict with all that is unholy, not only in the world around us, but more especially in ourselves. If we have peace with God, we must inevitably be at war with the world, the flesh, and the devil. Hence, Wesley appropriately includes in his hymn book a large selection of hymns "For Believers Fighting, Watching, Praying," and also "For Persons Convinced of Backsliding." For sometimes even soundly converted Christians fall away from true repentance and faith and need to begin again. But they can neither begin nor continue in their own strength. They must always look to Jesus and the power of his Spirit for salvation from beginning to end. And if they "backslide," it is to him they must turn in order to be restored.

O Jesus, full of truth and grace,
  More full of grace than I of sin,

Yet once again I seek thy face;
  Open thine arms and take me in,
And freely my backslidings heal,
And love the faithless sinner still.

Thou know'st the way to bring me back,
  My fallen spirit to restore;
O for thy truth and mercy's sake,
  Forgive, and bid me sin no more;
The ruins of my soul repair.
And make my heart a house of prayer.

Ah! give me, Lord, the tender heart
  That trembles at the approach of sin;
A godly fear of sin impart,
  Implant, and root it deep within,
That I may dread thy gracious power,
And never dare to offend thee more.[37]

There are many ups and downs on the Christian's pilgrimage through this mortal life, but there is never any need for despair. We may very well have no confidence in ourselves, but we can and should have every confidence in our Lord. If we have not, Wesley will help us to find it by singing and praying about it.

I am never at one stay,
  Changing every hour I am;
But thou art, as yesterday,
  Now and evermore the same;
Constancy to me impart,
Stablish with thy grace my heart.

Give me faith to hold me up,
  Walking over life's rough sea,
Holy, purifying hope
  Still my soul's sure anchor be;
That I may be always thine,
Perfect me in love divine.[38]

This does not mean that anyone can become an absolutely perfect *person* in this life. The perfection Wesley teaches is not the perfection of angels or of Adam "before the Fall;" it is *Christian perfection*. It means being as good Christians as God can make us before he takes us out of this sinful world into heaven. It does not mean freedom from all kinds of unintentional faults, defects, and failings; but it does mean such a surrender to the love of God in Christ that we never intentionally do or say, think or even feel, anything out of harmony with the mind and Spirit of Christ. Even a "babe in Christ," a beginner on the Christian way, is of course free from any conscious, wilful acts of disobedience to God; he does not commit outward sin. But the mature, the "perfect" Christian is freed also from inward sin, from evil thoughts and tempers, from all passions and desires that are contrary to love. If this seems impossible to us, Wesley insists that "all things are possible to him. That can in Jesu's name believe." Then he says:

The most impossible of all
  Is, that I e'er from sin should cease;
Yet shall it be, I know it shall;
  Jesus, look to thy faithfulness!
If nothing is too hard for thee,
All things are possible to me.[39]

Christian perfection is sometimes described by Wesley as "total resignation to the will of God"—what a modern evangelist might call "complete surrender." But unlike some modern evangelists (and some of his contemporaries also), Wesley does not ask for or expect any such completeness of surrender at the moment of conversion. On the contrary, he believes it rarely if ever happens so soon. In fact, as we have said, with most people it does not happen till they are on their death-beds; and even when it happens earlier, it often has to happen more than once before it becomes a quite settled state in this life. Those, therefore, who have, or think they have, attained to Christian perfection have no grounds for complacency. They have not attained it by any virtue of their own but only by the grace of God, and only as they depend, moment by moment, on the grace of God can they retain it. On the other hand, those who have not yet attained it, or have attained and lost it, need never despair so long as they are seeking it. God, who has begun a good work in them by forgiving their sins and giving them his Holy Spirit, will surely bring it in his own time and way to completion.

Thou who didst so greatly stoop
  To a poor virgin's womb,
Here thy mean abode take up;
  To me, my Saviour, come!
Come, and Satan's works destroy,
  And let me all thy Godhead prove,
Filled with peace, and heavenly joy,
  And pure eternal love.[40]

Jesus, the First and Last
On thee my soul is cast:
Thou didst thy work begin
By blotting out my sin;
Thou wilt the root remove,
And perfect me in love.

Yet when the work is done,
The work is but begun:
Partaker of thy grace,
I long to see thy face;
The first I prove below,
The last I die to know.[41]

"THE SPIRIT AND DISCIPLINE"

Salvation, as Wesley always insists, is God's work in us, not our own achievement. But how does God do this work? What does it mean for practical purposes?

The first thing to be said here is that, just as Wesley's Methodists shared the same catholic and evangelical faith as other Christians, so they shared the habit of Public and private worship, using the same means of grace as the rest of Christ's Church. The reading and hearing of the Word of God, participation in the gospel sacraments, the practice of private and corporate prayer, and fasting—these "ordinances of God" they found to be the chief means by which God's salvation is brought to us, his grace made available to us; and the use of these means was an essential part of the Methodist discipline.[42]

Here again, however, there were certain particular emphases that were characteristically though not exclusively Methodist. The importance of preaching, for example, was stressed as it has not everywhere been. I cannot find that Wesley anywhere speaks of preaching explicitly as a means of grace, but he holds that wherever the gospel of Christ is preached, "the kingdom of God is at hand" as certainly as when Christ himself first spoke those words; for our risen Lord is present, according to his promise, with those who preach in his name.[43] The Christian preacher speaks God's word, not his own; he is an ambassador of God, a co-worker with God.

God, the offended God most high,
Ambassadors to rebels sends;
His messengers his place supply,
And Jesus begs us to be friends.

Us, in the stead of Christ, they pray,
  Us, in the stead of God, intreat,
To cast our arms, our sins, away,
  And find forgiveness at his feet.[44]

There is great need of such preachers, and therefore we are taught to pray:

Convert, and send forth more
  Into thy Church abroad;
And let them speak thy word of power,
  As workers with their God.[45]

Thy only glory let them seek;
  O let their hearts with love o'erflow!
Let them believe, and therefore speak,
  And spread thy mercy's praise below.[46]

Another characteristic feature of the Wesleyan understanding of the means of grace concerns the sacrament of Holy Communion, the Lord's Supper. This sacrament, as Wesley sees it, is not intended only for those who are established in the faith, or even for those only who are converted. It is also a "converting ordinance," to which those may and should be encouraged to come who are not yet converted but are only seekers after true repentance and saving faith. Wesley himself led countless throngs of those who responded to his preaching in field or market-place to the Table of the Lord, in order that there they might meet the Saviour of whom he had been telling them.

Come, to the Supper come,
  Sinners, there still is room;
Every soul may be his guest,
  Jesus gives the general word;
Share the monumental feast,
  Eat the supper of your Lord.

In this authentic sign
  Behold the stamp divine:
Christ revives his sufferings here,
  Still exposes them to view;
See the Crucified appear,
  Now believe he died for you.[47]

How strange that among the successors of those first Methodists (and among other Christians, too) there are those who do not attend

Holy Communion because they are not "good enough"! As if anyone ever were or could be "good enough"! As if it were not for sinners that Christ died! It was indeed for sinners that he died, and both converted and unconverted sinners have perpetual need of him. They should therefore take every opportunity, as Wesley insists in his sermon on *The Duty of Constant Communion,*[48] of meeting him in the sacrament that he has ordained. There the crucified and risen Lord himself is present and presides, imparting to all who truly seek him a share in his own eternal and blessed life. As we approach his Table, we sinners may well say:

> Saviour, and can it be
> That thou shouldst dwell with me?
> From thy high and lofty throne,
> Throne of everlasting bliss,
> Will thy majesty stoop down
> To so mean a house as this?
>
> I am not worthy, Lord,
> So foul, so self-abhorred,
> Thee, my God, to entertain
> In this poor, polluted heart:
> I, a frail and sinful man;
> All my nature cries: Depart![49]

Yet as we come away, we can joyfully and thankfully confess:

> O the depth of Love divine,
> Th' unfathomable grace!
> Who shall say how bread and wine
> God into man conveys!
> *How* the bread his flesh imparts,
> *How* the wine transmits his blood,
> Fills his faithful people's hearts
> With all the life of God![50]

The Wesleys and their Methodists have no theory as to "the manner how" Christ is present in the sacrament; they only know from rich experience "the fact that" he is present, and they rejoice to meet him there.[51]

But besides the resources common to all Christians, the first Methodists had certain spiritual helps peculiar to themselves. There were short daily services on weekdays (at five in the morning and six or seven in the evening) with preaching, prayer, and singing; a Sunday morning service (beginning between nine and ten) that concluded with

Holy Communion and a Sunday evening meeting of the Society; the weekly "Class" Meeting; and a quarterly review of the members by the Wesleys or their Assistants, in the light of the conditions of membership. As we have said, anyone could become a member who sincerely desired to "save his soul"; but he must evince the sincerity of his desire by "avoiding all known sin, doing good after his power, and attending all the ordinances of God"; otherwise his membership would be terminated.[52] For, as Wesley held, "it was a true saying, which was common in the ancient Church, 'The soul and the body make a man; and the Spirit and discipline make a Christian.'"[53]

Out of this vital union of "the Spirit and discipline" there emerged five features which, though again not exclusively Methodist, became specially characteristic of the Methodist movement. They may be described as: Spiritual Fellowship, Lay Ministry, Active Evangelism, Social Concern, and what Wesley calls "Catholic Spirit."

(1) Spiritual Fellowship.

The Wesleys gathered their followers together, as we have said, into Societies. As they saw it, no man could find his way to heaven by himself, and Christians could not be isolated, solitary souls.

> Woe to him whose spirits droop,
> To him who falls alone!
> He has none to lift him up,
> To help his weakness on:
> Happier we each other keep,
> We each other's burdens bear;
> Never need our footsteps slip,
> Upheld by mutual prayer.[54]

Christianity, after all, is a religion of love; and not of self-love but love of one's brethren and neighbours in Christ. "Fellowship" has therefore always been a key word in Methodism, and in original Methodism it was much more than a word. In order to make and keep it a living reality, Wesley divided his Societies up into Classes. These were groups of not more than a dozen members, who met together once a week under the leadership of one of their own number for conversation on the spiritual life.

The Class Meetings were not study circles, not discussion groups, and least of all were they debating societies. They were Christ-centered fellowships. Their members were taught to take seriously our Lord's promise that he would be present in the midst wherever two or three were gathered together in his name. Hence, when they met in Class, they would sing:

> Jesus, we look to thee.
> Thy promised presence claim!
> Thou in the midst of us shalt be,
> Assembled in thy name:
> Thy name salvation is,
> Which here we come to prove;
> Thy name is life, and health, and peace,
> And everlasting love.[55]

Then they could go on to share their Christian experience with one another—their troubles and triumphs on the Christian way, or on their quest for that way. Sometimes they confessed their sins to one another, sometimes took one another to task, but always with the aim of helping one another to grow in grace, in faith and hope and love. Their varying degrees of spiritual maturity enabled them all the more to help one another by mutual conversation and prayer, and it was of course understood that no one ever gossiped about anything that was said in Class.

The purpose of the Class Meeting is perhaps nowhere better expressed than in these verses of Charles Wesley's:

> Help us to help each other, Lord,
> Each other's cross to bear,
> Let each his friendly aid afford,
> And feel his brother's care.
>
> Help us to build each other up,
> Our little stock improve;
> Increase our faith, confirm our hope,
> And perfect us in love.
>
> Then, when the mighty work is wrought,
> Receive thy ready bride:
> Give us in heaven a happy lot
> With all the sanctified.[56]

Always there is the perspective of heaven, both in John Wesley's preaching and in Charles's hymns. Always there is a goal ahead of us to be aimed at, a goal that has been reached by so many of God's people already, and by many known to us. Methodists used to be so accustomed to singing about heaven that they looked forward to going there and being reunited with their friends. "Our people die well," said Wesley, and for those who died he taught the ones who remained to sing:

Rejoice for a brother deceased,
  Our loss is his infinite gain;
A soul out of prison released,
  And freed from its bodily chain.

Our brother the haven hath gained,
  Out-flying the tempest and wind,
His rest he hath sooner obtained,
  And left his companions behind.

There all the ship's company meet
  Who sailed with the Saviour beneath,
With shouting each other they greet,
  And triumph o'er trouble and death.[57]

Not that heaven is a far distant place, nor are those who have reached it far separated from us who are still on the way. They are one with us in the communion of saints.

Let all the saints terrestrial sing,
  With those to glory gone;
For all the servants of our King,
  In earth and heaven, are one.
One family we dwell in him,
  One Church, above, beneath,
Though now divided by the stream,
  The narrow stream of death.[58]

Wesley's Methodists have a range of vision that is not bounded by the horizons of this world. But they are not otherworldly in the bad sense of having no concern for this world and its affairs, as we shall see.

(2) Lay Ministry.

In the Class Meeting, Methodism gave a practical demonstration of the Priesthood of All Believers. For the Leader of the Class, like its other members, was a layman—or woman. The Class was a group of Christian laity ministering to one another in holy things. Moreover, the Leaders of the several Classes in a Society were responsible for the spiritual oversight of the Society as a whole, and they exercised discipline in it under the direction of the minister, who was one of Wesley's "Travelling Preachers." These Preachers, whom Wesley appointed to serve in wide circuits throughout the United Kingdom and in distant America, were themselves also for the most part laymen; and so, too, were the "Local Preachers" who served when the Itinerant was away on his travels.

Methodism had a very high regard for the ordained ministry, but it had no room for clericalism. Clericalism arises from a secularised view of the laity, when men forget that the laity are the *laos,* or *People* of God, among whom the clergy are simply the duly appointed leaders—leading laymen in fact. Then the laity are regarded as "lay" in the sense of "not professionally qualified," while the clergy with their professional qualifications are allowed to claim a virtual monopoly of spiritual competence and responsibility. But in true Methodism there can be no such monopoly. It was not for preachers or leaders only, but "For Believers Fighting," that Wesley gave words like these to sing:

Shall I, for fear of feeble man,
The Spirit's course in me restrain?
Or, undismayed, in deed and word
Be a true witness for my Lord?

The love of Christ doth me constrain
To seek the wandering souls of men;
With cries, entreaties, tears, to save,
And snatch them from the gaping grave.[59]

Nor do the hymns "For Believers Working" have reference to "church work" only.

Forth in thy name, O Lord, I go,
  My daily labour to pursue,
Thee, only thee, resolved to know
  In all I think, or speak, or do.

The task thy wisdom hath assigned
  O let me cheerfully fulfil,
In all my works thy presence find,
  And prove thine acceptable will.[60]

And the hymns "For the Head of a Household" assign a spiritual task to both parents and employers:

Master supreme, I look to thee
  For grace and wisdom from above;
Vested with thy authority,
  Endue me with thy patient love:

That, taught according to thy will
  To rule my family aright,
I may the appointed charge fulfil,
  With all my heart, and all my might.

O could I emulate the zeal
  Thou dost to thy poor servants bear!
The troubles, griefs, and burdens feel
  Of souls entrusted to my care:

In daily prayer to God commend
  The souls whom Jesus died to save;
And think how soon my sway may end,
  And all be equal in the grave![61]

(3) Active Evangelism.

Methodism could not be other than an evangelistic movement. The gospel, the good news of salvation, as John and Charles Wesley had found it, had to be told. They could not keep it to themselves. Nor could thousands of others who found it through their ministry. Very fittingly, therefore, the first hymn in their hymn book was:

O for a thousand tongues to sing
  My great Redeemer's praise,
The glories of my God and King,
  The triumphs of his grace!

Look unto him, ye nations, own
  Your God, ye fallen race;
Look, and be saved through faith alone,
  Be justified by grace.[62]

It was the Aldersgate experience and the knowledge of Christ he received there that led John Wesley to say, "I look upon all the world as my parish,"[63] and Charles to write:

O for a trumpet voice,
  On all the world to call!
To bid their hearts rejoice
  In him who died for all;
For all my Lord was crucified,
  For all, for all my Saviour died![64]

Methodism began as a mission to the lost sheep of the Church of England,[65] for whom the Wesleys prayed:

Jesu, thy wandering sheep behold!
  See, Lord, with tenderest pity see
The sheep that cannot find the fold,
  Till sought and gathered in by thee.

Thou, only thou, the kind and good
  And sheep-redeeming shepherd art:
Collect thy flock, and give them food,
  And pastors after thine own heart.[66]

They also prayed for the clergy, the ordained priests and pastors of the flock:

Jesu, the word of mercy give,
  And let it swiftly run;
And let the priests themselves believe,
  And put salvation on.[67]

But Methodism could not limit its concern to the Church of England, or even to the English nation. The Wesleys had been brought up in a missionary-minded home; they had been—briefly and unsuccessfully, it is true—missionaries themselves; and above all, they knew that the gospel of God was the message for the whole world. So Methodists were given hymns to sing "For the Heathen" and "For the Jews" and for the entire race of men.[68]

(4) Social Concern.

Together with evangelism and missionary outreach, there went hand in hand social concern. It is true that when the early Methodists met in Class or Society they would sometimes sing:

In Jesu's name, behold, we meet,
Far from an evil world retreat,
  And all its frantic ways;
One only thing resolved to know,
And square our useful lives below
  By reason and by grace.

But the next verse of the hymn reminded them, if they needed it, that Christians are not called to turn their backs on the world in its need but to minister to it:

Not in the tombs we pine to dwell,
Not in the dark monastic cell,

By vows and grates confined;
Freely to all ourselves we give,
Constrained by Jesu's love to live
The servants of mankind.[69]

Wesley told his people that God had raised them up, "Not to form any new sect; but to reform the nation, particularly the Church; and to spread scriptural holiness over the land."[70] He also told them that "Christianity is essentially a social religion"[71] and that there is "no holiness but social holiness."[72] For holiness means love, the love of God and one's neighbour, which cannot but move us to seek to do all possible good to all mankind. Moreover, while ministering to men's souls is of primary importance, there are also temporal and material needs of men that must be met in the Spirit of Christ.

Thy mind throughout my life be shown,
While listening to the sufferer's cry,
The widow's and the orphan's groan.
On mercy's wings I swiftly fly,
The poor and helpless to relieve,
My life, my all, for them to give.[73]

Wesley's own social concern was actively manifested in innumerable ways. We recall, for example, his tracts and sermons on the use of money and possessions; his pamphlets against smuggling, bribery at elections, intemperance; his plea for government action to deal with unemployment and the high cost of food;[74] his support of the anti-slavery campaign; his opening of medical dispensaries for the poor; his educational enterprises; his orphanage; and his home for aged widows—to mention no more.[75] And he sought to teach his people,

By word and by deed,
The bodies in need,
And souls to relieve,
And freely as Jesus hath given to give.[76]

In these ways, no less than in his preaching of sermons and building up of his Societies, he saw the fulfilment of his vocation:

To serve the present age,
My calling to fulfil:
O may it all my powers engage
To do my Master's will![77]

(5) "Catholic Spirit."

This is the final mark of all true Methodism and one that is stamped on every aspect of it. In his sermon under this title,[78] Wesley defines it as "catholic or universal love." It is love for God and all mankind, especially our fellow-Christians. It is the antidote to the sectarian spirit that he attacks in a companion sermon entitled "A Caution against Bigotry."[79] Wesley's Methodism is the sworn foe of all sectarianism.

This does not mean that Wesley objected fundamentally to the existence of different Christian denominations. He believed them to be inevitable—in a fallen world. We cannot all think alike, and therefore we cannot all worship alike. There are bound to be diverse expressions of the Christian faith and life. What is more, each of us is bound to think his own denomination the best there is; otherwise, we would presumably not belong to it. But there is a difference between believing our own to be the best and believing it to be the only right one. That is sectarianism; that is bigotry. It means in effect that we equate our way of seeing things and doing things with God's way, as if the work of God could not be rightly done, if done at all, in any other way. Against this attitude Wesley warns us, reminding us of our Lord's rebuke to his disciples when they told him they had forbidden a man to cast out demons "because he followeth not with us."

Charles Wesley also castigates this attitude in brief but telling terms:

> Ye different sects, who all declare,
> "Lo, here is Christ!" or, "Christ is there!"
>
> Your stronger proofs divinely give,
> And show me where the Christians live.
>
> Your claim, alas! ye cannot prove,
> Ye want the genuine mark of love.[80]

Here is the essential point, the one thing needful: "the genuine mark of love." Without this you may well have a sect but not the true Church of Jesus Christ.

This is the whole substance of Wesley's sermon on "Catholic Spirit," for which he takes as his text Jehu's words to Jehonadab in II Kings 10:15: "Is thine heart right, as my heart is with thy heart? . . . If it be, give me thine hand." Wesley is here preaching no mere heartiness nor even that "religion of the warm heart" which is sometimes supposed to be Methodism. He certainly holds that the state of a man's heart is more important than his theological opinions or mode of worship, but it is with the rightness rather than the warmth of the heart that he is concerned. A catholic spirit is more than mere cordiality. Jehu's words in Wesley's sermon mean (in brief): Do you believe in Jesus Christ and in God through him, and does your faith lead you to love God and your neighbour—every man—as Christ has commanded? If so, or if you are sincerely seeking to have it so, then give me your hand. That is to say, accept me as your brother in Christ; pray for me, provoke me to love and good works, join with me in the work of God as far as ever you can.

In a letter to a brother clergyman in 1763, Wesley wrote:

> I am not satisfied with "Be very civil to the Methodists, but have nothing to do with them." No; I desire to have a league offensive and defensive with every soldier of Christ. We have not only one faith, one hope, one Lord, but are engaged directly in one warfare. We are carrying the war into the devil's own quarters, who therefore summons all his hosts to war. Come, then, ye that love him, to the help of the Lord, to the help of the Lord against the mighty![81]

In this same warfare Christians of all denominations (if they know their business) are perpetually engaged, and there was never more need for unity among them than today. Let each, then, be as attached as he will to his own opinions (whether liberal, conservative, or neo-orthodox) and as devoted to his own mode of worship (Anglican or Free Church, Catholic or Protestant); but let him be still more clear that the most essential thing about Christians (unless they are merely nominal Christians) is not their denominational allegiance or theological position but simply the fact that they are Christians—members of Christ, children of God, and therefore friends and brothers of his own.

Christ, our Head, gone up on high,
Be thou in thy Spirit nigh:
Advocate with God, give ear
To thine own effectual prayer!

One the Father is with thee;
Knit us in like unity;
Make us, O uniting Son,
One, as thou and he are one![82]

Sweetly may we all agree,
Touched with loving sympathy;
Kindly for each other care;
Every member feel its share.

Wounded by the grief of one,
Now let all the members groan;
Honoured if one member is,
All partake the common bliss.

Love, like death, hath all destroyed,
Rendered all distinctions void;
Names, and sects, and parties fall:
Thou, O Christ, art all in all![83]

Notes to Introduction

I. DISCOVERY OF A MESSAGE

[1] *CWJ*(J)I.82 = *CWJ*(T) 134f. [24 Feb. 1738].

[2] CW explains "the harmless nickname of Methodist" as due to his and his friends' resolve "to observe the method of study prescribed by the Statutes of the University." (See Frank Baker, *Charles Wesley as Revealed by His Letters* [London, 1948], p. 14.) JW gives a fuller account in S.132 (W.VII.421): "The regularity of their behaviour gave occasion to a young gentleman of the College to say, 'I think we have got a new set of Methodists'—alluding to a set of Physicians, who began to flourish at Rome about the time of Nero, and continued for several ages. The name was new and quaint; it clave to them immediately; and from that time, both these four young gentlemen, and all that had any religious connexion with them, were distinguished by the name of *Methodists.*"

[3] *JWJ*.I.109 = W.I.17 [14 Oct. 1735].

[4] *JWJ*.I.143 = W.I.2 [25 Jan. 1736].

[5] *JWJ*.I.151 = W.I.23 [8 Feb. 1736].

[6] *JWJ*.I.471 = W.I.101f. The "imminent danger of death" to which JW refers was occasioned by a storm at sea, the latest of a series on both the outward and the homeward voyages, which made a deep and lasting impression on him.

[7] *JWJ*.I.442 = W.I.86.

[8] *JWJ*.I.454 = W.I.91 [22 Apr. 1738].

[9] *JWJ*.I.471f. = W.I.102 [24 May 1738].

[10] *CWJ*(J)I.88 = *CWJ*(T) 142 [17 May 1738].

[11] *Ibid.*

[12] Martin Luther, A *Commentary on St. Paul's Epistle to the Galatians,* ed. P. S. Watson (Winchester, N.J., London, 1953), pp. 177f. and 179f.

[13] *CWJ*(J)I.95 = *CWJ*(T) 153 [24 May 1738].

[14] *JWJ*.I.464 = W.I.96 [21 May 1738]. JW adds: "His bodily strength returned also from that hour."

[15] *JWJ*.I.475f. = W.I.103 [24 May 1738].

[16] *Works of Martin Luther, Translated with Introductions and Notes* (Philadelphia, Pa., 1932), VI.449f. and 451f.

[17] *JWJ*.I.476 = *W*.I.103.

[18] *W*.VIII.367. Cf. *JWJ*.I.454f. = *W*.I.91.

[19] *HPCM* 30; *MHB* 361; *WHB* 35.

[20] *L*.V.258: to the Countess of Huntingdon [19 June 1771].

[21] *W.*VIII.300 (large Minutes). The date 1737 stands in the original text, though one might have expected 1738.

[22] From 1725, when he first read Thomas à Kempis' *Christian Pattern* (*The Imitation of Christ*) and Jeremy Taylor's *Rules of Holy Living and Holy Dying*. See *L.*IV.298f.(=JWJ.V.117; W. III.212f.): to John Newton [14 May 1765]; cf. also *W.* VII.421 (S.132).

[23] In this they are not so different from Luther as is often supposed. For Luther himself can say: "If there is not love, neither is there faith, but mere hypocrisy" (*Luthers Werke,* [Kritische Gesamtausgabe, Weimar, 1883ff.], XXXVI.474, 10f.). And see my article on "Luther and Sanctification" in the *Concordia Theological Monthly,* Apr., 1959, and "Wesley and Luther on Christian Perfection" in the *Ecumenical Review,* Apr., 1963.

[24] The material in this section consists of extracts from *CWJ*(J)I.92-123=*CWJ*(T) 149-94.

[25] *HPCM* 22; *MHB* 193; *AMH* 136. Samuel Wesley senr.

[26] *HPCM*(S) 786. Isaac Watts.

[27] *HPCM* 231; *MHB* 874; *WHB* 2 ("A Birthday Hymn").

[28] The material in this section consists of extracts from JW's *Journal* and *Letters.*

[29] *JWJ.*I.476-84W.I.103-6.

[30] *JWJ.*II.70-97W.I.158-63.

[31] Cf. *JWJ.*I.415f.=W.I.72, where JW confesses himself "convinced of unbelief."

[32] *L.*I.262ff.=*W.*XII.33f.

[33] JW frequently records the fact, without comment, that his preaching proved unwelcome to the church authorities, and he was told he would not be allowed to preach there again. This happened even before Aldersgate, and before he preached salvation by faith. "It was for preaching the love of God and man that several of the Clergy forbade me their pulpits before that time," he says in *L.*II.65=W.XII.70: to "John Smith" [30 Dec. 1745].

[34] *JWJ.*II.125-73=*W.*I.170-85.

[35] *HPCM* 279; *MHB* 783; *WHB* 124. Johann Joseph Winckler (1670-1722), tr. by JW.

[36] *L.*III.308f.=*W.*IX.36: to Dr. Lavington, Bishop of Exeter [Dec. 1751].

[37] *L.*VI.153=*W.*XII.284: to Miss March [9 June 1775].

[38] *L.*VII.319=*W.*XIII.52: to Elizabeth Ritchie [24 Feb. 1786].

[39] *L.*V.15f: to his brother Charles [27 June 1766]. The words in double brackets were written in shorthand, as intended only for Charles's eye.

[40] *HPCM* 189; *MHB* 375; *WHB* 31.

II. FULFILMENT OF A MISSION

[1] *W.*VIII.350.

[2] By "Primitive Church" JW means what to-day we more commonly call the "Early Church," particularly the Church of the first three centuries, the Church of the Ante-Nicene Fathers.

[3] *L.*VIII.224f = *W.*XIII.119: to Dr. Pretyman Tomline, Bishop of Lincoln [26 June 1790]. Cf. *L.*VIII.231 = *W.*XIII.126: to William Wilberforce, a Member of Parliament, [July 1790]. Had the Methodists applied for a licence as Dissenters, there would have been no trouble. They were refused it because they were members of the Church of England. Then they were threatened with starvation by the outrageously heavy fines imposed on them.

[4] *L.*III.192 = *W.*XIII.167: to Samuel Walker [3 Sept. 1756].

[5] *L.*II.289f. = *W.*XIII.493f.: to Dr. Gibson, Bishop of London [11 June 1747].

[6] *W.*XIII.195f. ("Reasons against a Separation from the Church of England," 1758).

[7] *W.*XIII.233: "Let them hold particular or general redemption, absolute or conditional decrees; let them be Churchmen or Dissenters, Presbyterians or Independents, it is no obstacle. Let them choose one mode of baptism or another, it is no bar to their admission. The Presbyterian may be a Presbyterian still; the Independent or Anabaptist uses his own mode of worship. So may the Quaker; and none will contend with him about it. They think and let think. One condition, and one only, is required—A real desire to save their soul" ("Thoughts upon a Late Phenomenon," 1788).

[8] *W.*VIII.352 ("Advice to the People Called Methodists," 1745).

[9] *L.*VIII.211: to Thomas Taylor [4 Apr. 1790].

[10] *W.*X.352 ("Remarks on a Defence of Aspasio Vindicated," 1766).

[11] *L.*V.155: to Professor John Liden [16 Nov. 1769].

[12] *L.*I.285f.: to James Hervey [20 Mar. 1739].

[13] *L.*III.150f. = *W.*XIII.176f.: to Thomas Adam [13 Oct. 1755].

[14] *L.*II.77f. = *W.*XII.79f.: to "John Smith" [25 June 1746].

[15] *L.*III.182 = *W.*XIII.179: to James Clark [3 July 1756].

[16] *L.*IV.110 and *JWJ.*IV.418f. = *W.*III.24f.: to the Editor of *Lloyd's Evening Post* [17 Nov. 1760].

[17] *W.*XIV.353; *MHB* (v).

[18] See his massive treatise on the subject, *W.*IX.191-464 ("The Doctrine of Original Sin according to Scripture, Reason and Experience," 1756-57). See also below, pp. 80-90.

[19] *HPCM* 93. JW also speaks of himself as having been a Pharisee—*JWU.*III.61 = *W.*I.409.

[20] *HPCM* 6; *MHB* 327; *AMH* 191.

[21] *HPCM* 6.

[22] *HPCM* 80.

[23] *HPCM* 400; *MHB* 87; *WHB* 69.

[24] *HPCM* 5; *MHB* 311.

[25] *HPCM* 10.

[26] Cf. *L.* VI.297f. = *W.*XII.33f; *W.*VII.336 and IX.194; and below, pp. 80-81, 88-90.

[27] *HPCM* 39; *MHB* 75. (Italics mine.)

[28] *HPCM*(S) 707; *MHB* 188; *WHB* 91.

[29] *HPCM* 105.

[30] See below, pp. 119-126.

[31] *HPCM* 96; *MHB* 377; *AMH* 208.
[32] *HPCM* 198; *MHB* 420.
[33] *HPCM* 205; *MHB* 406.
[34] *HPCM* 391; *MHB* 562; *WHB* 41.
[35] *HPCM* 363.
[36] *HPCM* 417; *MHB* 559.
[37] *HPCM* 186; *MHB* 346; *WHB* 20.
[38] *HPCM* 183.
[39] *HPCM* 401; *MHB* 548.
[40] *HPCM* 413.
[41] *HPCM*(S) 674; *MHB* 105.
[42] See below, pp. 157f.
[43] *W*.V.81 (S.7) = *SS*.I.155 (S.7: "The Way to the Kingdom").
[44] *HPCM* 11.
[45] *HPCM*(S) 745; *MHB* 787; *WHB* 122.
[46] *HPCM*(S) 744; *MHB* 791; *WHB* 121.
[47] *HLS* 8. On this whole subject see J. Ernest Rattenbury. *The Eucharistic Hymns of John and Charles Wesley,* in which the entire collection is reproduced, together with JW's Preface extracted from Brevint's *Christian Sacrament and Sacrifice.*
[48] *W*.VII.147-57 (S.101). When he reprinted this sermon in 1788 JW added a prefatory note, saying: "The following Discourse was written above five-and-fifty years ago, for the use of my pupils at Oxford. I have added very little, but retrenched much; as I then used more words than I do now. But, I thank God, I have not yet seen cause to alter my sentiments in any point which is therein delivered."
[49] *HLS* 43; *MHB* 760; *WHB* 142.
[50] *HLS* 57; *WHB* 147.
[51] We shall meet the distinction between "fact" and "manner" again, in connexion with Wesley's exposition of other doctrines of the Faith.
[52] *W*.VII.209 (S.107: "On God's Vineyard").
[53] *W*.VII.411 (S.131: "The Work of God in North America"); cf. *JWJ*.III.491 = *W*.II.204.
[54] *HPCM* 487.
[55] *HPCM* 485; *MHB* 718; *AMH* 25; *WHB* 5.
[56] *HPCM* 503; *MHB* 717; *AMH* 419. Concerning the origin of the Class Meeting, see *JWJ*.II.528 = *W*.I.357 [15 Feb. 1742]; *W*.VIII.252f. ("A Plain Account of the People Called Methodists"); *W*.XIII.226 ("Thoughts upon Methodism"); and *W*.XIII.276 ("A Short History of the People Called Methodists").
[57] *HPCM* 49; *MHB* 973.
[58] *HPCM*(S) 949; *MHB* 824; *AMH* 422; *WHB* 104.
[59] *HPCM* 279; *MHB* 783; *WHB* 124.
[60] *HPCM* 324; *MHB* 590; *AMH* 290; *WHB* 54.
[61] *HPCM* 470.
[62] *HPCM* 1; *MHB* 1; *AMH* 162; *WHB* 1.
[63] *L*.I.286—quoted above, p. 32.

[64] *HPCM* 34; *MHB* 114.

[65] *W*.XIII.195: "An the first message of all our Preachers is to the lost sheep of the Church of England" (Reasons against a Separation from the Church of England").

[66] *HPCM*(S) 744; *MHB* 791; *WHB* 121.

[67] *HPCM* 446.

[68] *HPCM* 444-49 are for the Heathen, 450-52 for the Jews. *MHB* 794 and 814 are missionary hymns written by JW and CW respectively.

[69] *HPCM* 526.

[70] *W*.VIII.299 (Large Minutes).

[71] *W*.V.296 (S.24) =*SS*.I.382 (S.19: "On the Sermon on the Mount, IV").

[72] *W*.XIV.334 (Preface to Hymns and Sacred Poems, 1739).

[73] *HPCM* 364; *MHB* 605.

[74] *W*.XI.53-59 ("Thoughts on the Present Scarcity of Provisions").

[75] Wesley would thoroughly have approved the idea of the Welfare State, with its policies of full employment, universal health and retirement insurance, and so forth.

[76] *HPCM* 495.

[77] *HPCM* 318; *MHB* 578; *AMH* 287; *WHB* 51.

[78] *W*.V.492ff.(S.39) =*SS*.II.126ff.(S.34).

[79] *W*.V.479ff.(S.38) =*SS*.II.104ff.(S.33).

[80] *W*.VIII.43f. (where the entire hymn is appended to "An Earnest Appeal to Men of Reason and Religion") =*HPCM* 16 (which, however, omits the second of these two verses); and WHB 118.

[81] *L*.IV.218=*W*.XIII.209: to Henry Venn [22 June 1763].

[82] *HPCM* 517.

[83] *HPCM* 518; *HHB* 720; *WHB* 111.